Under A
Buttermilk Moon

Spring plowing

UNDER A BUTTERMILK MOON

A Country Memoir

ROY WEBSTER

With an introduction by
Sally Chandler Crisp

August House / Little Rock

Published 1984 by August House Inc., P.O. Box 3223, Little
Rock, AR 72203. 501-663-7300

Manufactured in the United States of America

Library of Congress Cataloging in Publication Data:
Webster, Roy, 1913-
Under a buttermilk moon.

1. Webster, Roy, 1913- 2. Arkansas—Biography.
3. Arkansas—Social life and customs. 4. Country life—Arkansas.
I. Title.
CT224.W43   1985   976.7'05'092484-71805
ISBN 0-935304-78-9

First Edition 1985 hardback only

ISBN 0-935304-78-9

Cover design by Madeline Collins
Production artwork by Ira Hocut
Design direction by Ted Parkhurst

Evelyn Webster

This little book is dedicated to

Evelyn

the girl I searched for in my boyhood,
the girl I found in my early manhood,
the girl I married at 21,
the one who has shared my heartache and despair,
my achievement and victory,
the mother of our three fine children: Harold,
Dale and Helen.
The four . . . my greatest treasures.

CONTENTS

INTRODUCTION

It all started, according to Roy, with a paper route. It was the early 1930's, and eager to get out of farming, where fortunes depended on the weather, Roy took a 125-mile newspaper route for the *Southwest American* out of Ft. Smith. Soon he decided he might as well be carrying more than just the paper and worked out a deal to deliver bread for the Harris Baking Co. along the same route. While these two enterprises did not exactly make him rich, there was enough money coming in so that he and Evelyn could get married. So Evelyn became Roy's partner—and in more ways than one. She decided she could bake pies for Roy to sell on his route. And in the winter of 1934-35, Evelyn baked and Roy delivered 17,000 two-crust pies to grocery stores in Avoca, Brightwater, Garfield, Seligman, Gateway, Pea Ridge, Elm Springs, Cave Springs, Tontitown, and Lowell. Next they were selling butter and then chocolate milk!

When at the end of the 30's a bakery in Rogers became available, Roy and Evelyn went into the bakery business.

Roy discovered Evelyn had a talent for cake decorating and sent her to Chicago to study with a "master." Soon the Webster Bakery was catering fine weddings and other occasions for, as Roy puts it, "people of substance" all over northwest Arkansas. The bakery business was good as the war came on: sugar was being rationed, and people found fruitcakes were just the thing for mailing to soldiers. But would their business continue as strong after the war? Roy decided he needed an idea. What resulted was a gift package: a small wooden chest (with a padlock and a key) containing a 1½-pound fruitcake and ceramic jugs of sorghum and honey. "Rare Gift of Arkansas" they called it. Accompanying it was a booklet discussing the hickory nut and detailing the stories of sorghum and honey. Soon "Rare Gift of Arkansas" found a market with commercial buyers. The next year it was another product and another booklet for the same customers and more. (The stories in this book first appeared in these booklets.) Over the years, Roy and Evelyn have come to feel that the booklets and the philosophy therein may be as important as the products they accompany. As Roy puts it, "We sell a philosophy and throw in the jelly."

What is Roy Webster's philosophy? First, it is the belief that the "good old days"—despite the hardships—were indeed good. As Roy remembers them, the good old days were full of good people, good work (from sun to sun and hard, of course), good food (lots of it), good experiences. Roy recalls going to the train station to meet soldiers returning from World War I, grinding coffee at Mr. Rice's store, stuffing a pig into a gunny sack, harvesting wheat, having the preacher to Sunday dinner, starting school in the one-room Mason School, milking and churning and sometimes making ice cream, going to the County Fair, getting a telephone, and many, many more things. And he remembers the good-ness of these times with warm feelings and appreciation—but

10

without phony sentiment.

"Faith, hope, love . . . but the greatest of these . . ."— here, too, is Roy Webster's philosophy. Raised by parents rich in faith, hope, and love, Roy has a fine inheritance. He writes of times when these were all they had to survive on, and survive they did. Indeed, faith and hope, as Roy sees it, were as essential as sunshine and rain to his parents' success in farming that Ozark hillside. And love abounds in these stories. There is family love evidenced in cooking and sewing and teaching—as his mother redeems a winter work day with the promise of candy-making in the evening, as she sews shirts for the first-grader-to-be, as his father helps him and his friends build their own log cabin. There is also love for neighbor: his parents' leaving their house open so that the mountain people could use the telephone, his mother's accompanying the doctor to care for those reclusive folks, his father and mother's sharing of "fresh meat" when hogs were slaughtered, his many apples for the teacher. For Roy, faith, hope, and love are not abstractions; they are concrete: faith is a harvest of strawberries, hope is a new stove, love a patchwork quilt.

But, while this book is filled with philosophy, it is not a book of philosophy. It is a book of life, of personal history (how we need such stories to be written down!), of a time and a place, yet of every time and any place. Most of all, it is a pleasure; it is laughing, it is remembering, it is learning, it is delighting in Roy Webster's voice and spirit.

Finally, this book is a celebration. I'm glad I was invited to be a part of it; you'll be glad you came, too. Happy Anniversary, House of Roy and Evelyn Webster!

Sally Chandler Crisp
Little Rock, Arkansas
June 1984

11

Huckleberry, summer grape, deer, wild turkey, big timber wolf—all resisted the advancement of mankind here.

OUR HOMESTEAD

Now faith is the substance of things hoped for, the evidence of things not seen.

—Hebrews 11:1

It took a lot of Hebrews 11:1 to launch a future on a rocky, forty-acre hillside farm covered with sage grass, sassafras sprouts and big timber . . . surrounded with three rusty, zig-zagging barbed wires stapled to trees that "were almost on the line" and to an occasional fence post.

It was the spring of 1918 that old Molly pulled the first wagon load of our earthly possessions through the gap and stopped in front of a dilapidated one-room cabin that represented the intentions and failures of the previous owner.

The cabin, half-hidden with second-growth brush and wild blackberry briars, a "box" type about 14 x 16 feet, had been built a long time ago of 1 x 12 inch oak boards nailed upright to 2 x 4 stringers that ran around the crude frame structure. Homemade clapboard shingles were nailed to two-way rafters that came nearer providing shade than shelter. The cabin was lined with split, water-stained oatmeal paper tacked to the wall with big-headed tacks. Cobweb-bordered windows and a plank door let the light in and the heat out or in, depending on the time of year. The rough 1 x 12 plank floors had cracks wide enough for two-way passage of dust . . . down with a broom and up when the wind blew under the cabin. They showed signs of heavy boots, lye soap, and scrub water.

The cabin was adequate indeed for our possessions. Mom's black, four-hole, skinny-legged, cast iron cook-stove . . . had already been a cookstove for a long time. A cupboard (sometimes called a "safe") with several coats of time-checked paint and varnish had metal perforated panels in the doors and sides. Our "dinette set" was a rickety, reconditioned style with unmatched legs, two squeaky chairs with nail heads showing, and a tall goods box. The iron bedstead, once a gold color, would have a brand new wheat straw mattress and sheets and pillow-cases that bore the faded trademark of Gold Bond and Town Crier flour, and some very pretty pieced quilts. The remainder of our belongings included two light fixtures (a coal oil lamp and a coal oil lantern), an old trunk, a cast iron skillet, a black bread pan, a tea kettle, a water bucket with a tin dipper, a handful of utensils, three place settings of unmatched china and silverware, and a wardrobe that could best be described as a change of clothes for three.

Our second wagon load represented our capital investment in equipment: an old ten-inch Oliver turning plow with new handles, a double shovel, a single stock, one section of a springtooth harrow, a wooden smoothing drag, a revolving grinding stone, a grubbing hoe, two garden hoes, a garden rake, a post-hole punch, pitch fork, a scythe, two axes, a shovel, and a few hand tools, our hunting gear, a .12-gauge, double-barrel Stevens shotgun and a .22 single-shot rifle. And finally three coops of hens, and a 40-pound pig. A jersey cow, that was going to have a calf "right away," was tied to the back of the wagon with a rope, bringing up the rear.

Dad and Mom saw eye-to-eye on the great possibilities of that rock farm; they were self-reliant, independent, tough, and durable—and poor. They knew that $10 an acre was big money for land and the $350 mortgage would be burdensome, but they hadn't the slightest doubt about the outcome: they knew they could get rich growing strawberries, and they intended to grow lots of them.

Mom and Dad stretched both ends of daylight with a lantern. They cleared the land . . . grubbed, plowed, and planted oats, corn, sorghum cane and two acres of strawberries that year. It was a test of strength and ingenuity. When asked how they had done it, the answer was simple . . . you would have to do it to understand.

Mom picked, dried, canned, and cured everything that could be chewed and swallowed. The .22 rifle and an unerring aim furnished young rabbits and squirrels for the summer. The hens converted green grass and bugs into more eggs than we could eat; we had some to sell. Old Jers spent her time changing green leaves, sprouts, and grass to milk—enough of it for her calf and us. The pig rooted his way to over 200 pounds by fall.

During the summer, the chickens roosted in a wild plum thicket and ran under the cabin floor when it rained. Old Jers ranged the place with a bell around her neck. The pig was kept in a pole pen that was moved every day or so. Old Molly ate her grain from the end of the wagon box and rested between jobs in the shade of a red oak tree.

That fall Dad traded work and saw logs for enough oak lumber to build a shed for Molly and Jers, a chicken house for the hens. Now they could live in luxury too. Only the pig had a dismal future; about the time he thought he had it made, the end would come.

By the first snowfall the corn was shocked, the oats were stacked, the potatoes were "holed up." And Molly, Jers, and the hens were in shelter. Best of all though, two acres of fine strawberries had made it too. The wide rows were full of healthy plants ... plants that would, barring frost or drought, bring reality to Mom and Dad's dreams next spring.

As winter closed in, the problem of comfort became acute. After the sun had shone and the wind had blown a few days, the clapboard shingles would shrink. Then when it rained again, they would leak like a sieve until they "swelled up" ... but by then it was too late; everything would be wet. And there was the problem of sifting snow. The cabin was as cold inside as outside when the fire went out at night. The snow would stay on the floor 'til morning; then the King heater would melt the snow and everything would be damp again.

You have a gap in your life if you have missed trying to sleep in a ceilingless cabin with an all-night rain pattering on a clapboard roof, then running through and dripping into a menagerie of pots and pans. Every so often the leaks would shift ... then miss the pot or pan ... so you spent the night moving the pots and pans under the changing leaks. But it was a symphonic sound that would make a lifetime impression.

We had central heating in the summer ... direct from the sun; central air conditioning in the winter too ... direct from the north pole. We had running water also: a spring about 500 yards down a steep ravine. We never went to bed without a full water bucket and tea kettle just in case of fire. We had ice in the house ... around the air holes where our breath escaped through the folds of the heavy quilts.

It took unlimited motivation and raw courage to hit

that cold floor every morning . . . barefooted, especially if you left tracks in a skift of snow.

As winter wore on, Dad spent his long days clearing more "new ground" for another strawberry patch . . . made fence posts, saw logs, and firewood out of the timber. Mom patched, darned, knitted, read her Bible and tried to "make ends meet." At night we sat close to a red hot King heater and built air castles. Mom envisioned a painted house . . . three rooms maybe . . . kitchen, front room, and a bedroom with pretty wallpaper and linoleum rugs . . . a well of water close to the house. Dad's imagination ran in a different direction. He could see another horse to help Molly, two-horse tools, another cow, more chickens, a good barn, new orchards, a vineyard, and bigger and better strawberry patches. He dreamed and banked on a big strawberry crop next year.

January, February, and March of '19 were tough and severe, tested the endurance of everything. The chicken combs froze and turned black . . . egg laying dropped off. Jers' milk production waned a little, too. Molly's hair grew long and shaggy.

(The gloom of war had spread over the earth. The *St. Louis Globe Democrat,* our only contact with the outside world, came twice a week . . . it told of the Kaiser and all the trouble "over there.")

The ground hog failed to see his "shadder" . . . so we could expect an early spring. Sure enough it was. A warm sun and gentle showers brought a new outlook. Dad whistled as he worked; Mom hummed and sang "Amazing Grace" over and over as she planted an early garden. The hens cackled with joy as they dusted themselves of chased bugs and scratched for worms. Molly and Jers enjoyed the tender grass and began to shed their winter coats.

April 1st Dad found the first strawberry blossom; a few days later the vines were in full bloom. We lived in constant fear of frost and drought; if the sun shone all day, we were sure it was the beginning of a drought. When it rained or the wind changed, we were sure it would freeze or frost before morning, but as each day went by, the prospect of frost diminished; finally only drought or hail could alter our future. The first few days of May were warm and humid. Dad found the first ripe strawberry May 5th. On May 9th aunts, uncles, and cousins converged on the strawberry patch for the first pickin'. The vines were loaded with big berries and a hot sun made them grow and turn red fast. In 15 to 18 days the crop had come and gone.

Strawberries were a festive crop . . . the first cash crop for the year in the Ozark Mountains. And there were so many wonderful ways to benefit from them.

It would be hard to explain what went on in the minds and hearts of Mom and Dad when they hauled the first pickin' of their own strawberries to town on that memorable day in the spring of 1919, but it was easy to see the smiles of achievement. They had battled the elements and the weeds; they had matched raw courage against deprivation; they had mated hard work and ingenuity with hope . . . and won. The victory was sweet, and they were enjoying it.

The two acres of strawberries produced enough cash to pay for more barbed wire, the interest, a few new clothes, another horse, taxes, $150 on the mortgage, a pretty $3.95 linoleum rug and enough screen wire for the door and windows. A couple of years later, Dad built a new four-room house . . . two rooms upstairs and two downstairs with a connecting ladder.

Dad never got rich growing strawberries, but he was a good strawberry man and had an undying faith in them . . . had a patch every year for as long as I can remember.

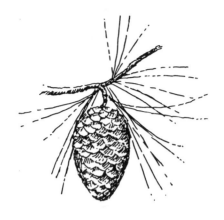

THE LOG CABIN

Every log house and cabin is a monument to the everlasting ingenuity and determination of the first immigrants to the new world. Their motives were many, their goals were varied, their vision untarnished; they were armed with an unwavering faith that penetrated their gloom and discouragement. They would reveal the rainbow beyond as they began to push back a stubborn frontier, chopping, sawing, planting, and building their way across 4,000 miles of uncompromising land.

Log cabins built on the frontier by the first settlers were for shelter only. Comfort and convenience were all but unknown and never expected. If they could be dry and nearly warm, that was enough. If they were camping in the open or housed in a covered wagon, the constant threat of rain, storm or blizzard gave great urgency to the building of a log cabin. Once the logs and pole rafters were on the cabin site, the neighbors would often arrive for a log raisin' (sometimes a surprise). Sometimes the ladies would serve dinner on the ground. In a day or two the folks would move in. As prosperity came, a "lean-to" would be added, built of additional logs or lumber. When water power was developed along creeks and rivers and lumber began to appear, wood floors too would be added; the split pole door and leather hinges would be replaced with sawed lumber and metal hinges. Eventually glass would replace the wood-covered windows.

The log cabin pictured on the following page was an outgrowth of another cabin my cousin Virgil Volk and I built of small poles on the banks of Job's Pond in 1923. The next year we built a larger cabin with old logs that came out of an old log barn. Both were major undertakings with great success in the eyes of two small boys. We enjoyed basking in our achievements as we played around the cabins for a long time.

In the spring of 1925, Teed and Shorty Hoover moved into our lives when their parents bought the Kelso farm near us and moved to it from somewhere a long way off. The Kelso farm was a romantic place to me . . . about 100 acres of hills, ravines, springs and saw log timber. Virgil and I decided it was our duty to meet and welcome Teed and Shorty to our neighborhood. They beamed when we showed them our log cabins. After a few days entertaining Teed and Shorty around our log cabins, we discussed building another, larger and better, log cabin big enough for four of us on the Kelso place. The idea created instant enthusiasm. Mr. Hoover listened to our plans and thought it was a great idea and seemed excited when he gave us permission—but only after we agreed when we cut each log we must cut the rest of the tree into stove-length heating wood and burn the brush. (It was already easy to see it would take a lot of biscuits and jelly to fuel the project.) We chose a beautiful site on a grass-covered, V-shaped ridge between two deep ravines. The cabin would be about 10 x 12 feet . . . facing east with two tall yellow pines near the two front corners overlooking

Our log cabin

a 200-foot deep ravine that began near the east-west graveled road . . . went south about ¼ mile then joined the other ravine and headed toward the river. The upper end had a large spring bubbling up out of a bed of limestone rocks that formed a small, crystal-clear lake about 100 yards long, 25 yards wide, about seven or eight feet deep surrounded by century old oaks that had traded their oak shade for the lake's life-giving water across the ages.

On Friday, March 21, 1925, the usual six-month school term had come to an end at our one-room Bellview School. Virgil and I had passed by the skin of our teeth, and we felt accomplished. Tomorrow, Saturday, we would face our largest undertaking to date—the log cabin—by selecting and blazing (marking) the trees we thought were suitable for the purpose. The higher the branches grew on the tree and the straighter the better. Teed and Shorty, as it turned out, were from Nebraska where many similar problems were solved by building "sod houses" from Buffalo grass sod. Since Virgil and I had so much experience in building, they would do everything they could do to help and follow our advice. Our 10 x 12 cabin would require 12 side logs 14 feet long and 12 end logs 12 feet long and about 12 inches in diameter. By noon we had blazed 24 trees. Virgil and I tried to use big words like professional log raisers did—such as broadaxe, cant hooks, crosscuts, double-bitted axes, notching, skidding, and so on. Teed and Shorty thought we were experts. Virgil and I gladly accepted the recognition.

That afternoon the log cutting began. We came armed with full stomachs, crosscut saws, axes, wedges, and mallets. Virgil and I pointed out the tree must be notched on the same side we wanted it to fall, and I demonstrated by using my axe to notch out the first tree. Then we sawed the other side with a crosscut saw; if the tree was leaning or a breeze blowing against it, the saw would soon pinch. Then we drove the wedges into the saw cut with a wood mallet, forcing the tree to fall the direction it needed to fall. It was much easier to cut the tree than to trim the log and cut the balance into stove lengths. Teed and Shorty caught on fast and were a big help. The log cutting lasted one and a half Saturdays.

Next in line was skidding the logs to the building site. We used ole Molly and Mae, our mares. They were gentle and patient which would come in handy with log handling. Since the butt ends of the logs were larger, they would be alternated while skidding into position to keep the walls level.

Well, it took two Saturdays to correct the site and place flat corner rocks for the cabin and get the logs ready. By now, all four of us were totally consumed in the cabin project. Every moment of every evening until dark and all day Saturday we toiled. Teed and Shorty proved that they were what they appeared to be. Our parents became great friends. Now it was a family project. Next Saturday would be the day of all days . . . the log raisin'. Our Dads said they wanted to help at least one day, and next Saturday we could use the extra help.

Saturday morning introduced a bright clear day which would be a scorcher—about 100 degrees. Our Dads with cant hooks, Molly and Mae with a long wire cable and four eager boys, whose teeth were chattering with excitement, arrived at the site about sunup. Getting 12 wall logs and 12 end logs raised, providing for the door and two windows, notched and in place all in one day was a serious matter. We were glad our Dads would help. After one side log was set on each side and one end log fixed on each end, two skids were placed on the side log. The next log would have the cable around the middle of the log, and, as Molly and Mae pulled the cable, the log would roll up the skids. Uncle Frank and Mr. Hoover would keep it even with their cant hooks until it was in place. Just as we were finishing the third log high, here came Mrs. Hoover, Mom and Aunt Lucy in a buckboard drawn by a glossie, coal-black mare. They stopped on a flat place in the shade of a big oak near the cabin and spread a tarpaulin on the ground and a pretty tablecloth on the tarp . . . then a big roaster with fried chicken, a big bowl of mashed potatoes, chicken gravy. Aunt Lucy had fixed a gallon stoneware milk crock of leaf lettuce and sliced onion wilted with hot vinegar. Teed skidded down the ravine with a three gallon bucket and brought it back with ice cold water straight from the big spring. Mrs. Hoover made enough lemonade to last all evening. Mom opened a big jar of peach preserves and sliced two loaves of fresh home-made bread. There was no way we could eat enough to last a half day . . . but we tried.

I shall never forget that day: three families shaped from the same mold of love and appreciation for one

Homemade ice cream begins here!

another in the true spirit of the American frontier—and a log raisin'. The rest of the log raisin' went as planned until the last log was level. When the front log got to the top of the skids the log got loose and beyond our control, rolled across and fell off the cabin, and landed against the two pines in front of the cabin. As we surveyed the situation, it looked nearly impossible to move it. Shorty suggested we leave it there, floor it and make a porch. We all agreed it was the thing to do. So by accident we had a porch, and now we needed another log. In cutting our logs we found one tree that was long enough for two end logs. As it turned out we didn't need it for end logs, so we cut off about six feet and made a side log for the last log . . . at 6:00 p.m. on Saturday . . . one of the happiest days of our lives.

Next week we would work on the pole rafters and gable logs and string eight-inch boards on the rafters to nail down the clapboard shingles. My Dad helped; we found a nice water oak about 20 inches in diameter to make clapboard shingles. He said it was a shame we had to cut such a beautiful straight tree for only a few 24-inch cuts for shingles, but the sap was high in that tree and the shingles would split out nicely, would have a straight grain, be thinner, and make the cabin look nicer when they were finished. So the water oak was cut down. It was about 20 feet to the first branch, thus, nine 24-inch cuts. Teed and I sawed the nine cuts with a crosscut saw. Teed's experience in sawing the wall logs was a big help now. Each cut was barked and quartered. The adge, a tool for the purpose, had a blade about 12 inches long with a handle socket big enough for an oak handle about the size of the small end of a baseball bat. The blade would be set about ¼-inch or less from the edge of the cut and struck with a wooden mallet. After each lick the adge handle would pry the slice a little. We would strike it again and pry again until the slice hopped off the cut and became a shingle. The sap wood would be shaved off with bark to give the shingle a longer life. Once Teed and I caught on a little, we made shingles faster. By the time the shingles were made, the rafters, gables, windows and door arrangements had been made, and we were ready for shingles. The first course was doubled; then the next course had a 12-inch exposure and so on. With four anxious, squirrel-like boys on the roof, it didn't take long to get it done. The door and two windows were faced with rough oak and almost square; with a lot of whittling we made them fit.

The 2 x 6 floor joists rested on flat rocks with 1 x 12 inch planks for the floor nailed to the joists. It looked real good until the floor shrank and left one-inch cracks.

We were down to the chinking between the logs to keep the cold winter wind from blowing through. The 24-inch wedge-shaped scraps left from the shingle making were just the checker; we drove them in until they were tight.

The next task was a brand new experience. We sifted

red clay soil through screen wire and mixed in enough water to make a firm mud, then troweled it over the log chinking until it was well-filled and smooth. The mud made the cabin seem cozy inside!

The days were getting shorter and cooler. School time was drawing nigh about the same time the cabin was livable. We had spent most of the summer's spare time at the cabin. Our parents quizzed us . . . when would we move in? They seemed excited, too.

A secondhand, long, flat-top heating stove with a hearth and a six-inch stovepipe going straight through the ridge row were set up and added warmth and charm. Our furniture was an up-ended apple box, seats of three old cane-bottom chairs reinforced with baling wire; an old drop-leaf table turned out to be useful as long as we kept a small block under the one leg. Aunt Lucy gave us a pretty kerosene lamp. Shorty framed a picture of Tom Mix and Tony, his horse, and hung it on a nail. While Virgil and I finished the two-deck, two-passenger bunks with a connecting ladder, Teed made curtains out of burlap sacks which read "100 LBS. OF MIXED FEED" and had a small picture of two cute calves . . . it was funny to us.

We drew straws to see which two were to sleep on the top deck of the double bunk. Virgil and I drew the privilege. At first we thought it was great, but when it rained, the shingles would leak like a sieve until they swelled up . . . by then the bedding was soaked.

Monday morning the teacher announced that there would be no school Friday due to the County Teacher's Meeting. So Friday night, October 10, 1925, we would have our first supper and first night in the new log cabin. Mom suggested she could make us a big kettle of vegetable soup with crackers and a pitcher of milk. We voted that Teed would have the honor of fixin' our first breakfast of homemade sausage, eggs, and toast made in a greasy skillet.

The next five days seemed like an eternity, but Friday finally came ... movin' day ... quilts, pillows, books, dishes, forks, knives, and spoons. When we fixed the beds, they didn't look like our Moms had done it, but they did look inviting.

While Teed stoked the fire, Virgil set the table; Shorty went after the milk and crackers at his house, and a little after five I came with the soup. As I walked through the door and saw the fire burning and the glow of the kerosene lamp, I was never so proud of anything in my life. We had made everything with our own hands. Teed's and Virgil's eyes were sparkling with delight. I put the soup on the stove; while it heated, we simply sat and grinned at one another ... hardly knowing what to do next.

It was altogether possible that we were four of the happiest boys on earth. So we ate the best vegetable soup in the world that night. After supper Virgil and Teed washed the dishes while Shorty and I carried two armloads of wood onto the porch.

The remainder of the evening we discussed our future. We had used some of Zane Grey's, Harold Bell Wright's, Jack London's (and other western authors' and heroes') ideas in the planning of our vast empire. That night in our imagination we envisioned thousands of acres of land . . . great cattle herds . . . large apple orchards, peach orchards and strawberry fields and hundreds of employees—operating the whole thing straight from our log cabin headquarters.

For almost three years this delightful fantasy played an important role in our four lives. Then one day Mr. Hoover made a "tragic" announcement; with a solemn and almost regretful voice, he said they had sold the farm and bought a Studebaker automobile dealership in another town ... they would have a sale soon.

As time went on, all four of us knew the reason we had been encouraged to build the log cabin and all the heartwarming experiences that went with it; it was the wisdom and desire of our parents to help us form a base on which to build character ... a lesson in creativity, vision, and imagination ... to develop the tenacity, determination, and the muscle to support our ideas and objectives.

A TIME FOR SHARING

Good ham and bacon for winter started on our 35-acre farm in the spring when our old Poland China sow had her spring litter. She averaged about eight pigs to the litter. By weaning time (eight to ten weeks), Dad could tell the good ones from bad, usually picked out three of the lar gest and most promising pigs to fatten and sold the rest . . . got two to five dollars a piece for them. Of course, the pigs didn't know, but they were eatin' themselves into trouble from that minute on. In spite of the eventual outcome, they lived a life of leisure all summer. They had a big trough of wheat shorts and water twice a day, a few ears of corn night and morning; the rest of the time they grazed on alfalfa or sudan grass and enjoyed a big mud hole in the shade of a large pecan tree.

The latter part of September they had moved up in their world. They were no longer pigs . . . they were shoats. In their new status they were confined to smaller quarters, getting less exercise and more feed. Actually they felt uncomfortably full at times.

About the tenth of October their status changed again. They were moved to even smaller quarters with a board floor and nice clean oat straw for a bed and an endless stream of big yellow ears of corn. The frosty autumn nights whetted their appetites and the yellow corn continued to taste good. The clean oat straw bed made their hair shiny and curly. They enjoyed their bed even more as the days went by. They no longer had a desire to romp and play, even when the weather changed. It was just more fun to lie on a full stomach and grunt with contentment.

The second or third Monday morning of November, the sun arose with a strong south wind; the air was heavy with blue wood smoke blowing in from big timber fires on the mountains across the river. Just before I left for school, I heard Dad tell Mom, "That wind will blow up something in a day or two."

That night I noticed a big pile of old posts, two wooden barrels, and two black, cast iron soap kettles had been unloaded under the large oak trees south of the barn.

At dawn Tuesday morning it was raining. Dad said I could wear my new rubber boots and walk to school but, if it kept raining, for me to wait at school that evening and he would be after me in the buggy. However, the rain stopped about noon, the wind changed from the south to the north, and the air began to get cold fast.

When I got home that night, the two oak barrels were under the eaves of the barn full of rain water. The two black kettles were sitting with each leg on a big rock high enough to get the old post under them. There were six or eight gamble sticks notched and ready, leaning against the tree. A large pole with one end in the crotch of a big limb and the other end resting in the crotch of two poles criss-crossed and chained together, probably eight feet high. This I knew would be used to hang the dressed hogs.

On the back porch, several knives and a cleaver had been sharpened to a dangerous edge; the .22 Stevens rifle, cleaned and oiled, was standing near the water bucket. It was plain to see what would happen tomorrow. I learned from Mom that Uncle Frank and Aunt Lucy, as well as Mr. and Mrs. Jenkins were going to butcher with us . . . about nine or ten head altogether. It would take most of the day. This meant that Virgil, my cousin, would come to our house after school tomorrow.

The three big hogs, on the board floor bedded with the bright oat straw, seemed disappointed that night when they failed to get their usual yellow corn and squealed their protest in no uncertain terms.

When I awakened the next morning there was plenty going on. A yellow light was flickering on our newspapered wall. It was the light from the old post burning under the black kettles. The steam was billowing from the warming water. I could see Dad in the light of the burning post arranging one of the oak barrels at an angle against an improvised platform that would be used to scald and scrape the hogs. Two rusty buckets filled with green wood ashes from the heating stove would be used instead of lye to make the hair slip.

In the dim light of dawn the heavy frost looked like snow. Uncle Frank and Mr. Jenkins were there quite a while before sunup. They looked at the hogs. Mr. Jenkins guessed 320 pounds average. Uncle Frank guessed 325 pounds. Dad had a modest guess of 295. All three guesses were safe because there was no way of ever knowing.

Dad picked up the .22 rifle and asked if they were ready. Uncle Frank, with a long bladed knife in his hand, nodded. Dad turned to me and said, "Beat it," and I did. A few minutes later I heard the crack of the .22.

When Virgil and I returned from school that evening, most of the butchering was over. Mr. Jenkins was just leaving with his meat in the wagon. It had been a big day, but the next few days would be, too: hams, shoulders, and middling to be trimmed and rubbed down with salt, sugar and pepper, head cheese to make, sausage to grind, feet to pickle and lard to render.

It was an old custom of the mountains and one that Dad and Mom enjoyed most: the remembering of the neighbors with a "mess" of fresh meat. There were always some deserving neighbors that needed help, then the neighbors who hadn't butchered yet (we sorta secretly hoped they would pay us back when they butchered), our pastor and his family, Doctor Gullege, and Mr. Carns, the mail carrier; Dad said it was a great blessing to share with our neighbors. It was worth all the effort just to see the expression of joy and appreciation on the faces of the folks.

EPOCH OF THE
ONE-ROOM SCHOOLHOUSE

The bleak one-room log schoolhouses of colonial days were a product of a freedom-starved people. A common people, lean from oppression, armed with a musket and an undaunted courage, willing to cast aside all the old world customs and face an uncharted ocean and a trackless land to start a new way of life. A folk determined to release their children from a rigid class yoke that they themselves were born under but were unable to escape except through the transition from hand-hewn logs to lumber or masonry.

The passing of time changed the style of the one-room school but little, though its general appearance usually reflected the stubborn pride and prosperity of the district.

We are indebted to the selfless and devoted teachers of that era, who walked miles upon miles through all kinds of weather for $20 to $50 per month to teach and janitor, who helped shape the mighty precepts which are still the very foundation of this freedom-loving America.

Much could be said about the contribution made by the authors and the publishers of McGuffy's, Harper's, and the Indiana Series Readers, Webster Blue-Back Spellers, Ray's Arithmetic and the Reed-Kellogg Grammar, to name only a few, written in a vein to develop a self-sufficient, independent, and inventive individual with far-reaching vision.

I would like to see a movement started to preserve the remaining one-room schools . . . a memorial to remind us of our great heritage.

I remember it all started at our house the fourth Saturday in August, 1919. The hot, sultry morning was spent about as usual, trying to finish everything that was started on our 40-acre, timber-covered, hillside farm during the past week.

Just before noon, Dad let Molly, our dapple-gray mare, into the barn. While she enjoyed three big ears of bright yellow corn and a fork of bushy-headed oats, he curried and brushed her real good, giving considerable attention to her beautiful mane and tail. Then, with justifiable pride, he draped her with a strong smelling set of oily black leather harnesses. Old Molly, usually a gentle horse, always laid her ears back, showed her teeth and gnawed the stall partition when Dad put the crupper under her tail. Then Dad and I pulled the one-seated top-buggy covered with a week's accumulation of cobwebs, dust, hen feathers, and straw from the barn and dusted it off as best we could.

Ordinarily, right after dinner (12 noon) Dad would hitch old Molly to the buggy, Mom would draw the cream and eggs from our dug well (our refrigerator), while I gathered the last-minute eggs from the hen house. However, this particular Saturday morning had one notable exception: we had to catch a few hens. In spite of some carefully laid economic plans made earlier in the summer, the money that was needed this Saturday was considerably short. So some Rhode Island Red hens had to span the gap.

With the cream and eggs in the boot of the buggy, the hens in a gunny sack with their beaks wide open and panting were shoved under the seat. Mom, laced to the limit in her new corset, sat on one side of the seat, Dad sat on the other side with one foot dangling down the outside of the buggy, and I sat on a plank just back of the dashboard. We were off to town on a rough road with dust ankle deep.

Molly hated automobiles and strange dogs with a purple passion. Nearly every settler along the road had at least one dog, sometimes several. They were a constant menace to the serenity of our trip to town.

This Saturday, about the middle of the five-mile distance, we met an automobile. It dashed by us at a breath-taking speed of at least 25 miles an hour. The driver was stiff and aloof as usual . . . this characterized all drivers of that day, we thought. Molly shied off the road into a shallow ditch crammed with sumac, sassafras sprouts, and blackberry vines, covered with a summer collection of dust and harboring thousands of grasshoppers. The dust was stifling and we almost smothered; after the dust settled, we got Molly back on the road. Mom complained, said between the sweat and the dust, we would look like tramps by the time we got to town. Dad threatened the hen's lives if they didn't hush the cackling, and he spent the balance of the 2½ miles saying some awful unpleasant things about the automobile, the man, and his wealth. Mom and I listened in sympathetic silence.

Once in town, my folks discovered a lot of other parents were getting ready for school too ... so we wound up milking late that night.

I don't remember the amount of money involved in my first school outfit, but even at the time I was aware, in a measure at least, of some of their sacrifice. Like most parents, my folks wanted their little boy to have everything, and in that I agreed. We soon discovered, however, there was a lot of difference in everything and what I got. But my supplies did include an Indian Chief tablet, a slate, a box of crayons, two pencils, a primer, a book satchel, and a round tin dinner pail. My wardrobe included enough of two kinds of striped material for four homemade shirts, a blanket-lined blue denim jacket with a corduroy collar, a stockin' cap (now known as a toboggan), two suits of long-handle underwear with a flap across the seat that buttoned (they finally stretched so much they would have fit a boy twice my size), three pair of knee-length black stockings, a pair of heavy Star brand shoes that had hooks instead of eyes (they turned green and smelled terrible when they got wet, got so stiff you couldn't bend them when they dried ... after my going barefooted all summer, this proved to be a real problem). Our earlier plans had called for three pairs of overalls but because of the hot, dry weather the hens didn't weigh out as much as planned; so we settled for two pair.

The following week was a big round of wonderful experiences for me. While Mom made my shirts, I put on and took off my new clothes several times, wore my new shoes until I had blisters and skinned places all over. (I went to school barefooted 'til frost, waiting for them to heal.) I nearly smothered wearing my new jacket and stockin' cap around the house. I had never had so many

*Arrow indicates the author among schoolmates
in 1919*

nice things all at one time.

September 8th was the day, exactly 6 years, 1 month, and 1 day after the stork brought me, I started to school. (It was not until 22 years later when our own son, Harold, started to school—September 15, his sixth birthday—that I fully understood what made my folks look and act as they did that September morning.) They smiled and said they were "real proud of me" and cried all at the same time.

The morning was cool, but the day would be hot and dry. It was decided, over my protest, that it would be too hot for me to wear my stockin' cap and denim jacket. Since my feet were too skinned up to wear my Star brand shoes, it would look better if I didn't. With a new striped shirt and new overalls, I looked good anyway. Armed with this assurance and with my book satchel strapped over one shoulder, my tin dinner pail filled with left-over chicken from Sunday dinner, a peanut-butter-jelly sandwich, a fruit jar of home-canned peaches and two cookies, I was ready to meet the issues and ordeals that were required to "edgicate" a son . . . long before Myrtle and Velma, my cousins, came by.

My dog, Carlo, sensing the approaching change at our house, barked as he spied Myrtle and Velma emerging from the sassafras and sumac-lined path that led from their house to ours. Mom said they were "pretty as pictures" . . . they had new clothes too.

"Be careful" and "be good" were the last words we heard as we disappeared into the gloom of the heavy timber. Our trip was interrupted when we discovered old Carlo following. A severe scolding and three or four well-aimed rocks changed Carlo's mind about going to school that day.

From our house, the walk to Mason School was down a long, long, long hill, past two spooky, uninhabited, and dilapidated log cabins, through the deep shadows of big virgin timber, across two creeks on foot-logs, four farms and past six or eight mean-looking dogs, and only the bravest small children could be expected to make it.

Mason School, facing east, sat in a scattering of red oak and white oak trees, sprinkled with a few hickories, near the mouth of a short, narrow ravine and sorta overlooked a big bend in the river that hugged close to the high, overhanging limestone cliffs on the far side to form a broad, fertile valley that was farmed by the Hearns, Alleys, Egans, Myers, and the McKinneys.

This morning, a low, early fog, which had since risen, made the dust in the dim road damp and cool to my bare feet. Fresh fox tracks at each end of the foot-log, the tracks left by a covey of quail and a black snake as they crossed the dusty road were familiar to country kids, but two pair of fresh, clean tracks—one pair with shoes, the other barefooted, going the same direction as we were— were a bit of a mystery, unless they belonged to the teacher and George Alley. The warm morning sun, breaking through thin layers of rising fog, was already coaxing the odors from the corn silks and new mown hay. A soft, gentle breeze was freighted with the sounds of lost calves bawling, lowing cattle, lonesome horses nickering, a boastful rooster crowing, ambitious hens cackling, a woodpecker impudently hammering on a dead snag with rivet-hammer rapidity.

As we approached the school ground, the toll of the 8 o'clock bell greeted us. It was the most inspiring sound I had ever heard, coming through the dark shadows of the big oaks from a bell sheltered in an open belfry that straddled the moss-covered roof of the old school-house.

Constructed of lumber, the school was a big building to me (maybe 26 x 30 feet). Its weathered siding had been painted at least once. It had three windows on each side and a door in front under the belfry.

A summer's growth of ragweed, dog fennel, sassafras, sumac sprouts, dewberry and sawbriar vines had been cut, raked and burned, leaving the odor of stale smoke and ashes plus the cruelest "stobs" and stray briars a little barefooted boy ever walked on. Most of my first recesses and noon hours were spent patching up my sore feet and digging out briars. Drinking water was carried by the bucket from the Egan place. A long-handled dipper with a hook on the end had been the fountain for everybody in the past, but this summer a well had been drilled and a long-handled pump put in. An unsightly pile of heating wood had been unloaded on the ground near the corner of the school so it would be handy.

I harbored mixed feelings as I stepped through the door for the first time; I was glad I was big enough to go to school, but I wasn't sure I was big enough to solve the problems. Miss Meeker's nice smile and friendly way didn't give me the answers, but they gave me the assurance I needed.

This morning, the blackboard was clean, the floor was mopped with all-but-fragrant floor oil. The walls were still unpainted. Bracketed kerosene lamps with reflectors were between each window. The teacher's crude desk was on a platform in the middle of the front end or the back end of the school—whichever you wanted to call it—at least it was on the opposite end from the only door. A big clumsy-looking pot-bellied stove sat in the middle and a little to the rear of the building. The fly-specked bailing wire nailed to the ceiling, stuccoed with paper wads, supported several joints of rusty stovepipe that fit into a bracket flue just over the teacher's head.

Big pictures of George Washington and Christopher Columbus were hanging on the wall back of the teacher's desk. Two rows of double desks in two sizes were on each side of the room with one row in the middle as far back as the stove; most of the desks bore the scars of Barlow knives and the carved initials of budding romances of each passing school term. A varnish-checked organ, with several ivories missing and the rug covering on the pedals worn threadbare, sat between the corner and the first window on the south side. Four glass ball-and-claw feet supported a squeaky organ stool that was supposed to match the old organ.

The nine o'clock bell rang and all the kids took their seats but me. I didn't know where to sit. I found out later if you wanted a certain seat, you had to get there early on the first day. Miss Meeker sized me up real good and decided it would be best for everyone if I took a front seat. One of the first and perhaps the greatest lessons I learned the first year was who was boss . . . and it wasn't me!

Some of the kids said their big brothers would start as soon as crops were finished, and sure enough they did. Two of them had mustaches and were as old as Miss Meeker. I heard Dad tell Mom they probably wouldn't

40

come if they weren't sweet on the teacher.

I depended on my cousins for security the first few days of school. After all, I was a little boy in a big world and away from home. But sharp ridicule and being referred to as a "sissy" prompted me to move from the girls' department over to a man's world right away.

I had the urge to be on the winning side at a very early age. I soon learned that, aside from giving my very best, my chance of winning was often determined by whose side I was on. In a game where speed was important, I wanted on Buck's side; in a game requiring accuracy, it was Albert's side. A ciphering match, it was Wilbur's side, and in the case of spelling, it was Nancy's. In choosing up sides, my outcome was decided early . . . it depended which one of the folks got first choice. There was one boy whose ability wasn't considered as good as mine, so I was always chosen next to the last one.

There was enough open space on our school ground to play "work-up" baseball, "blackman," "dare base," to pitch horseshoes, and a couple of places were worn smooth enough eventually to shoot some marbles. The girls jumped rope, played hopscotch, and a few other games we men folks didn't want to know too much about.

The middle of November found 19 enrolled and big plans for our first big program . . . Thanksgiving. My piece was all about being grateful for what we had and being generous with the less fortunate. On the big night I staggered and stumbled through all eight lines and sat down weak from fright. My folks smiled an approving smile and the rest applauded, and I vowed I'd play the leading role in the main play when I got big.

For several weeks I overheard the big kids discussing how big and important the Christmas programs were in the past, but not until Monday after Thanksgiving did Miss Meeker announce her plans. Nineteen of us sat wide-mouthed and bug-eyed as she revealed the details . . . it was almost too good to be true! Some of the older girls would copy parts, but some parts could be clipped and pasted on sheets on paper. Bed sheets for sliding curtains would be borrowed. Bathrobes for the wise men were abandoned in favor of blankets when it was discovered there was 'eer-a bathrobe in the whole community. And an alert was sounded: everybody on the lookout for a beautiful cedar tree just the right size. Nineteen of us applied for the curtain pulling job, and 17 of us had hurt feelings when Miss Meeker selected Burt and Opal, the only two seventhgraders we had.

All was forgiven and forgotten though when we drew names Thursday morning, a week or so before the magic night. This triggered another big experience . . . trading names. A feller traded my name for a pretty girl's name and gave a good Barlow knife to boot. There were several other trades of less importance made too, but all a little on the sly. My folks frowned on the practice, said it wasn't right. I believed them.

Thrills ran up and down our spines and our ecstasy was uninhibited when Miss Meeker announced contact with Santa Claus had been made and he would be at the school the night of the program to see that we all had treats. It was rumored there might be an orange in our sack of treats . . . if we had done our best in the program. A new wave of cooperation swept the school; new efforts to memorize parts were evident. Miss Meeker insisted on more expression and less tune in our pieces.

Finally all the paper dresses and angel wings were made, all the costumes arranged for, and the curtains were up. The big boys had finished the stage for each side of the teacher's platform. We were ready for a fulldress rehearsal. Our teeth chattered with excitement. The next day we would start decorating the tree. Everything was working out except the old organ. The cold weather was making the bellows stiff and the keys sticky.

Country School Days

Backward turn backward
  Thru time if you will,
To the old country school
  On the top of the hill.
Life was quite simple
  Without rush and speed,
For the mill, church and school
  Filled the bulk of our need.
In summer and winter
  Thru rain, snow and hail,
We trudged off to school
  With our old dinner pail.
Our coats were hung up
  On a peg or a nail,
On the shelf just above
  Was that old dinner pail.
When study was over
  And reciting was done,
There was lunch to be eaten
  Then barrels of fun.
But wait just a minute—
  Go with me to lunch,
Out under the trees
  With the rest of the bunch.
No king, duke or queen
  Ever ate better fare,
Peanut-butter sandwiches,
  Hard boiled eggs and a pear.
Time has brot changes
  And more modern ways,
But I'll always cherish
  My country school days.

Rev. Wm. E. Master

Of course, we were so carried away by the occasion, no one noticed it but Miss Meeker. She solved the problem, however, by keeping the organ shoved up close to the stove.

The dawn of the big day brought heavy rains and mud everywhere. We were soaked by the time we got to school. By noon the wind changed, the temperature began to drop sharply. The rain changed to big, wet flakes of snow.

Inside the school though, the Christmas spirit had not been dampened. The Christmas tree—decorated with foil, icicles, buttery-yellow popcorn on a string, green and red paper chains, colored candles and the tip bending a little under the weight of a glittering star—was beautiful beyond description. Gifts, not to exceed 25¢, were making their appearance. We had rehearsed the program over and over again; our complete confidence was evident. Only Miss Meeker knew what a crowd might do to that confidence. At noon Miss Meeker said the weather was bad, so no one would leave the room except to go to the little buildings marked BOYS and GIRLS.

Most of the boys sat on the up-ended stove wood and ate their lunches around the glowing stove that was doing its best to keep up with the dropping temperature. Most of us could hear the water squashing inside our shoes, but a few had rubber boots and insisted on burning the heels on the hot stove.

It may be possible to forget certain portions of the three "R's" learned at a one-room school, but eating sweaty sandwiches from an air-tight pail in a room filled with the fragrant aroma of a cedar Christmas tree and the mixed odor of drying tracked-in mud, a fluff of wood smoke from an occasional down draft and shattered green oak bark, compounded with the musty odor of dripping coats (some with a trace of skunk) drying near the stove, plus the burning rubber heels will make an

44

impression that will last a lifetime.

At 1:00 o'clock, Miss Meeker stepped off the platform and stood in front of the recitation bench with her hands clasped in front of her with a certain poise I had not recognized before and a smiling voice that I'll never forget. She told us what a wonderful group of pupils we were, how fine our parents were. She spoke of her visits to most homes (she had spent the night in a few), and she told us how she appreciated our willingness to help in the affairs of the school and especially the Christmas program. She was sure Santa Claus would be here tonight... Oh! how we loved her. Now, we would rehearse the last time, we must perform without prompting, each must say his piece slowly and with expression. In the next hour and a half, with a degree of calm assurance and rigid precision, we unraveled the great drama ... with near perfection.

Four o'clock found several cold and impatient saddle horses and a few horses and buggies waiting to rush kids home and families back by seven or so. I was glad to see Dad and Molly waiting too. The wind was high and cold, the flakes were fine and drifting now, nearly three inches was sticking to the brush and high grass, and the roads were muddy and freezing. Molly's hoofs squirted mud and splashed the water as she pulled us along the narrow road. Her belly was caked with frozen mud; her warm body steamed from exertion by the time we got home. Three hours isn't long when you have to make a round trip, do chores, and get into your Sunday best ... but we made it.

The first glimpse of the dimly lighted school and the first whiff of wood smoke blowing in our direction sent thrills of joy up and down my spine. Dark objects moving on the light snow were folks unloading or taking care of the horses. Straw-filled wagons loaded with dads, moms, grandparents, aunts and uncles and kids wrapped up head and ears were arriving. One surrey

45

with side curtains was already there. Dad hitched Molly to a small tree and strapped a heavy quilt over her. Inside the friendly stove was already thawing the chill of the trip for the early comers. The soft mellow light of the sparkling clean kerosene lamps revealed the strong character lines in the anxious faces of these hardy people that knew so well the cost of freedom, that knew so well the price of independence, to whom the word *convenience* was unknown.

But tonight they were happy. Girls with red ribbons in curly hair and pretty dresses, slick-haired boys dressed like little men, squirming and wiggling on the front seats, distorted shadows dancing on the bed-sheet curtains betraying the motions of the older group as they prepared the stage for action . . . these were their sons and their daughters. And all this was enhanced by the fragrance of captive cedar and bright decorations.

The magic of the night deepened and a calm settled over the pupils and parents as curtain-time neared. Miss Meeker turned on all the self-control she possessed as she stepped from behind the curtain and announced Velma Ingersoll would give the welcome. Tension seized Velma and all eighteen of the rest of us. For the next hour and a half, unabated fear and excitement drove our pulses high, caused hearts to thump and teeth to chatter . . . but somehow we performed as if by divine appointment.

Miss Meeker was everywhere and everything at once, but always clear to give moral support when a young voice quavered. Everyone sang and enjoyed Christmas songs, which were carefully timed to drown the noise made while changing stage props. Anxious parents held their breath when their offspring appeared on the improvised stage to do or say his part. Smiles of relief would spread across their faces as the crowd rewarded a fine performance with generous applause.

Just as the last tones of "Joy to the World" filtered

through the windows into the cold night air, a squeaking door betrayed the arrival of Santa Claus. He was right there before my very eyes; for the first time I saw him. He was dressed and looked exactly like his picture . . . a jolly and happy fellow. Yes, he was just what I expected to see. I even shook hands with him. But he was a busy man. In a few minutes, with Miss Meeker's help, the gifts under the tree were given out, and Santa opened his big bag. There were treats for all of us . . . even the little kids that weren't going to school . . . and "surenuff" an orange. Just as suddenly as he had arrived he disappeared. But our faces were still flushed with joyous expectancy as we broke string and tore paper from the packages.

Miss Meeker's voice had an extra ring of sincerity when she told the folks what fine children they had and expressed her appreciation for their braving the storm and attending the program that night and wished them a "Merry Christmas and a Happy New Year." She asked Brother Myers to dismiss us . . . and it took him about 20 minutes to do so.

"Tragedy" occurred during the Christmas season though. Two smart-aleck boys planted the seeds of doubt about the Santa Claus business in my mind; eventually, of course, the whole myth exploded and Christmas was different after that.

The balance of the year was filled with many new, big, and some wonderful experiences. We celebrated or recognized every mile-post America had passed. Miss Meeker made special occasions out of all the great leaders' birthdays, dead or alive, made sure their names had special meaning.

Many of my lessons were painful: I sat on the teacher's desk facing the kids for fighting; I stood at the blackboard with my nose in a ring for whispering. I was genuinely whipped with a tree limb for sassing. But somehow, I lived through it all and passed . . . by a narrow margin.

My folks decided if they were going to "get ahead," they would have to leave the cabin and rocky hillside farm; so they traded for 35 acres of smooth upland with a painted house, went in debt for the boot. We had, sure enough, moved up. I would go to Bellview School now. After a while, Dad was elected to the school board, and Mom was elected president of the SIA (School Improvement Association). After Dad's two terms on the school board and Mom's three years as SIA president, Dad learned to temper his criticism and was more thoughtful and selective in what he had to say about local leadership.

My wife, Evelyn, taps my shoulder and says, "Your supper is getting cold." After 41 years, I had returned to childhood. I had attended my first year of school again. I had felt the sharp stubble under my barefeet. I had smelled the blue wood smoke. I had warmed myself by the stove. I had heard the toll of the bell. To my knowledge, there were no great earth-shaking leaders produced at Mason School that year, but we did learn a little about the art of living.

THE BEEHIVE

Dad and Mom thought Joe and Grace were about 20 years old when they bought the 60-acre Kelso place just a quarter of a mile east of our house. I well remember the day they moved in with their things. It was a miserably cold Saturday afternoon in mid-January. It had rained most of Friday, then the wind had changed to the north and grown colder by the minute, and the temperature had dropped to zero before morning. Dad decided that we would go and help them move their things into the house and help set up the stoves and beds and maybe cut enough wood for the night. Mom said they would be chilled to the bone after being in the cold all day; she would fix supper for them . . . maybe they would feel more welcome to our neighborhood.

The Kelso house was a two-room box type with lean-to porchs on the front and back, roofed with clapboard shingles, sitting on rock piers about 16 inches off the ground and floored with 1 x 12 oak boards with a sheet of tar paper between the joists and floor to keep the wind

49

from blowing up through the cracks. Although the house had never been painted, it was a sorta pretty place in summer when the lilacs, redbud, or the dogwood was in bloom, but that day it looked bleak and forbidding to me.

My first glimpse of Joe and Grace assured me that we had fine new neighbors. She was real pretty and had a contagious smile. Joe was big and raw-boned, seemed courageous, and had a movement that convinced me he could do anything he wanted to do.

It was so cold that we got acquainted in a hurry. Dad and I learned that they had been Mr. and Mrs. Joe McFerron for only a few days and this would be their first housekeeping experience.

Even if Joe and Grace had had everything they needed for two rooms, it wouldn't have taken long to unload and set it up, but there was a big difference in what they needed and what they had . . . so it didn't take long. I didn't see anything new except two or three quilts, a sheet metal heating stove, a few dishes and a pan or two. Everything else was secondhand or had been given to them by well-wishing relatives.

The small cast iron cookstove was very simple . . . just a little scrolling with the word *BUCK* molded into the iron in two or three places. The sheet iron King heater had $2.00 marked on it with white chalk. The iron bedstead had been painted many times; the last time it was a cream color, but some of it had chipped off. Some of the coils in the bed springs were leaning, but there had been some effort to repair them with baling wire. We covered the springs with an old quilt so the rough places wouldn't wear a hole in the new straw tick. The old unfinished drop-leaf table was solid but was stained in many colors in many places by many spills. Three chairs that had been repaired were almost alike. An ancient dish cupboard that was covered with time-checked varnish had two solid doors below and two open doors above with screen wire tacked on the inside; two fork and knife drawers with china knobs were between the top and bottom doors. An old dresser, whose spotted mirror had been wrapped in a quilt, had time-checked varnish, too. The rest of their belongings, including 40 or 50 dog-eared books, were in wooden boxes or rolled and tied with binder twine.

Their two spirited, dapple-gray mares with beautiful manes and tails and bowed necks were impatient from standing in the cold. Their legs were covered with mud, and muddy icicles were hanging from their bellies. Their leather harness was nearly new and trimmed with nickel-plated rivets, red and white celluloid rings, and brass-covered hames. The red-wheeled wagon had a green bed and spring seat with the word *Studebaker* printed about middle ways on both sides of the wagon bed.

Joe was unhitching the mares from the wagon when Dad and I headed for home to do our chores. Dad waved at Joe and said we would see them about five-thirty.

Mom was in her best form at times like this. That night our house was spick and span: she had filled the lamps, trimmed the wicks, and polished the lamp chimneys to a lintless sparkle, the table had our white (indeed, our only) tablecloth draped upon it. Our best lamp was between our only unbroken cream and sugar set. Supper was ready when Joe and Grace arrived. Mom had fried big slices of ham cut straight from the middle of a country ham, made cream gravy from the fryings, had drowned the mashed potatoes in melted butter, baked buttermilk biscuits to a golden dusty brown. A peach cobbler would be baked by the time we were ready for it.

Between being out in the cold all evening and the excitement of having new friends for supper, my teeth chattered for at least 30 minutes.

During supper Joe told how, at 16, he had worked for a big fruit farmer for two years for $17 a month and room and board. He had saved his money and bought his mares and wagon. Then for the last two years he had share-cropped and the land owner had furnished the implements. He had been lucky; he had good crops and made enough to partially pay for the Kelso place, and his Granddad had gone his note at the bank for the balance. Joe's folks had given them 16 hens and 2 roosters. Grace's folks had given them a fresh cow and her bull calf; they would bring them home as soon as the fences were repaired. And Grace's grandparents had given them two hives of bees.

Joe's and Grace's eyes sparkled when they told of their romance. It started at a pie supper at the Beaver Springs schoolhouse in Delaware County when Joe mistakenly bid her pie in at 35¢, thinking he was getting another girl's pie. They had known each other about a year when they were married.

After the dishes were put away, Joe and Grace revealed, with great enthusiasm, their plans for the Kelso place. They would clean up the old orchard, cut out the diseased trees and replant with cherry, apple, and peach. They would restretch the wire in the grape vineyard, rebuild the fences, set out strawberries, raspberries, boysenberries, develop as many new hives of bees as were necessary to carry out his plans for pollenizing his crops, have a big garden to do a lot of canning. They planned to buy some adjoining land as soon as they could.

That night from our window, Dad, Mom, and I watched Joe and Grace walk home in the light of their coal oil lantern. Mom said they were marching into the future.

I went to bed wide-eyed. I thought of the events of the day, how suddenly a new chapter in life could begin. I dropped off to sleep, not realizing what the future held for Joe and Grace and me.

When the neighbors spoke of Joe and Grace, I would hear statements like: they're smart, sweet kids, big ideas,

*A typical mountain blue-blood . . . a veteran
bee hunter*

good ideas, bright future, they'll do all right. When Joe
talked to Dad, I would hear words like *fertilizer, spray
material, grafting, pollenizing, cross pollenization, yield.* I had
heard the words before but not with as much authority.

As the days rolled into weeks and the weeks into
spring, Joe and Grace stretched each end of the day with
a lantern. They were working or reading every waking
moment. Every time I was in their house I found the dog-
eared books open, or markers sticking out of the edges
to mark a reference. The words were too big for me, but I
could understand some of the pictures. One book was
about grafting. Joe had spent a lot of time in late winter
and early spring studying this book and experimenting
with grafting in his orchard. I had watched him graft one
variety of grape vine on the root stock of another variety.
He grafted different varieties of peach branches on one
peach tree. He said there would be just as many varieties
of peaches as there were grafts.

When the first spring blossoms began to show up, he began to study a book on bees, pollen, and pollenizing. He carried the book in his hand and a magnifying glass in his pocket most of the time. He gave more and more attention to the two beehives. When the peach and plum trees began to bloom, he watched with his magnifying glass as the bees worked on the blossoms. He would put a net over his head and watch the bees go in and out of the hive through the glass.

Wild bees were the only kind of bees I knew about. I knew they made honey from flowers and stored it in hollow trees. I had been around bee tree hunting; I had helped bait and trail bees to the bee tree. I had helped rob and eat the honey, but those two beehives of Joe's were something else. So my admiration for Joe and my interest in bees kept me with Joe every time I had a chance. Dad said accusingly that I would donate more work to Joe than he could hire me to do at home. I overheard Dad tell Joe one time, "When you get tired of him, run him off."

One real warm April afternoon I was with Joe while he was admiring the full bloom of his apple trees and enjoying the mellow buzz of the bees working on the blossoms when suddenly and out of nowhere it started to rain. We scampered to an old fruit shed and, while the rain pattered on the old tin roof, he began by asking the question . . . where do bees come from? Then he spent the rest of the evening answering it. A honey bee is always a member of a colony numbering up to 60,000 or more. Bees do not have a "boss," but all work together in perfect harmony. All workers are undeveloped females; all drones are males. Drones serve for mating of the queen and nothing else. The queen is a fully developed female, with a little longer body, smaller eyes, highly developed ovaries and some other differences.

He paused an instant following a loud clap of thunder and raised his voice a little in competition with the rain beating on the old tin roof. The propagation is controlled entirely by the queen. The queen goes about the hive laying eggs in the cells to hatch workers, drones, and queens. There is no difference in the eggs of a worker and of a queen. To produce a queen, the egg must be laid in a queen cell which is a little larger. The drone is hatched from an infertile egg. The queen is fed "royal jelly" which is secreted from the bees themselves and is a marvelously nutritious substance full of fine food value and loaded with vitamins. The reigning queen is very jealous of her "rivals." She must not be allowed to get near a queen cell after the eggs are laid or near young queens. If two queens are allowed to meet, a furious battle will ensue and will end only when one or the other of the queens is stung to death. One of the workers' duties is to keep them apart until one of the queens, usually the older, is willing to abdicate with a swarm. No one knows just how or who makes this important decision.

Joe noted a pair of lizards on a 2 x 4 from the corner of his eye and tossed a stick harmlessly in their direction. They "ski-daddled" and he continued. Swarming is a natural tendency and as necessary to survival as laying eggs. Swarming is the method they use in starting a new colony. A prosperous colony may swarm several times in one summer. Each time several thousand bees with a queen will leave the hive to find a new home. At this time they load themselves with enough honey to last until they get located. When they leave the hive they make a terrific buzzing sound, frightening everyone but the experienced beekeeper (who knows that bees seldom sting while swarming). The swarm usually settles on a low branch or bush. Then the scouts are sent out to seek a new location, usually a hollow tree. Or, on rare occasions, they may decide on a deep crevice in a rock or cliff. The tree that is selected is solid but hollow. It is important that the tree leans a little to help support the comb. Once in the tree every worker gets down to business—cleaning, scouring, removing any particle of dust and polishing. Bees are immaculately clean. No disease-bearing bacteria is ever found in honey. When this job is finished, they set about sealing all cracks and openings but one. This is done with "bee glue," a gummy substance gathered from the foliage of trees. This new home must be completely water-tight.

Joe stepped to the edge of the fruit shed and gazed upward as if to check the rain, then pointed out that the next job for the new colony is the construction of large quantities of comb for storing of honey and brood (or young bees). To make comb, they need wax—beeswax. Several bees line up on the upper side of the new home, hanging by the feet. Other bees come and hang on these bees; others hang on them and so on until a wall of bees is suspended across the hollow of the tree. They remain in this position converting honey that is in their stomach into wax which exudes from between the scaly plates of their bodies. When a solid foundation is made, then the erection of a six-sided cell begins. These are made from beeswax also. The cells slope upwards slightly so the nectar from the flowers can be placed. The cells are wonderfully uniform except for the drones' and queen's cells which are irregular. The accuracy and precision represent miraculous engineering.

Joe seemed a little uncomfortable and spoke a little more delicately when he began to describe the mating of the queen bee. Only once in a lifetime is it necessary. She comes out of the tree and makes a few trial flights to acquaint herself with the ground and area about so she may find her way back. Then she sets out on the greatest flight of her life, the "mating flight." The mating of a queen can only be accomplished while in flight. While the drones and queen are in the tree or hive, they never pay the slightest attention to one another; but when she leaves the tree on her mating flight, she is immediately

The good life is determined by hard work, good management and pollenization by bees.

pursued by every drone in the colony, sometimes a hundred or more. Occasionally drones from a neighboring colony will join in. Generally the queen is not caught by one of them until she is high in the air and out of sight. In fact, only a few matings have ever been witnessed. The drone in the act of mating seems to explode with an audible pop and always dies in the act. The queen returns to the tree with parts of the male's viscera attached to her abdomen. This is promptly removed by a worker, and she goes directly into the tree and starts her egg-laying career. The queen now has 4 million sperm cells stored in her body, possibly more than she will ever need. In a short time the colony is running smoothly again and continues until another group of bees and another queen decide to swarm and go into another tree—so there is no end to the process.

Joe concluded by telling me that one pound of honey required 34,000 trips to the flowers, that the average life span of a worker bee was 14 to 15 days, that she rarely enjoyed the products of her labor, that most plants produced sugar in their fruit, seed, or the sap of the stalk, but the largest concentration of natural sugar was honey.

Then Joe's brow furrowed a little as he said there was doubt that man, his cow, or his horse could have survived on earth without the bee to pollenate his food crops. He pointed out that wind, though erratic, played an important part in pollenization too, but the bee would be there to do it better and when it needed to be done.

With a sweeping gesture of his big brown hand, he foretold how he would have beehives everywhere they needed to be around his orchards and vineyards. He was sure they would improve the quality and the yield of his fruit . . . and he could sell the honey as a cash crop.

The last rays of a setting sun were piercing the big black thunderheads to the east when Joe and I left the fruit shed that evening. I knew I would need a good excuse for being late getting home, but I thought I had one.

When I went to bed that night, I knew how Saint Paul felt when he sat at the feet of Gamaliel.

As the years rolled by, I watched the fruition of Joe's and Grace's dreams, visions, management, and hard work. They were known as the "harvesters." They never imposed their views on the neighbors, but were generous and shared their wisdom and understanding of nature with all those who sought it.

Mom said they were good to the Lord and the land, so the Lord and the land were good to them . . . and I always believed it.

The quilting bee was always the most reliable place to catch the latest news.

MOM'S THIMBLE

Much of my boyhood was spent wearing the knees out of blue denim overalls and the elbows out of homemade shirts. If I had worn shoes and socks the year around, the holes worn in the toes and heels of socks might have outnumbered the holes in overalls and shirts, but going barefooted from the last frost in spring until the first cold snap in the fall saved a lot of wear-and-tear on socks. When we wore holes in overalls, shirts or socks, we didn't throw them away anymore than we would have thrown our bare feet away just because the skin had been knocked off the heels or toes.

(As a boy I learned to walk on my heel while new skin grew to cover a skinned toe or on my toe while the hide grew back on a heel, but a real "tragedy" occurred when I had the toe of one foot damaged and the heel of the other injured. If you haven't tried walking on the heel of one foot and the toe of the other at the same time, you have missed part of your equilibrium training.)

The repairing of overalls, shirts, and socks goes by

different names. The modern term might be *recycling*, but when I was a boy, it was called patchin' and darnin'. Patchin' and darnin' required special tools, special skills, and special people, including a pair of scissors, a needle and thread, a favorite thimble, lots of small pieces of cloth that "almost matched" and a mother long on love, patience, and thrift . . . but short on time. Mom qualified in all areas . . . she was busy every waking moment.

In those days about everything we needed was home-grown, homemade, or we did without. Sometimes it was easier to save than it was to make; the words *save* and *thrift* were synonymous. To this very day, it is hard for me to throw anything away—regardless of how useless it may be.

Mom always said that patches on the knees and elbows were honorable but patches on the seat were dishonorable; seat patches were signs of laziness. She said this with such conviction and so often that I always felt guilty when I sat down, and the more comfortable the chair the more guilty I felt.

From early spring until late fall, there was rarely time for patchin' and darnin'—with all the setting hens and baby chickens to take care of, the garden to plant, weeds and insects to fight, strawberries and other fruit to pick, vegetables and fruit to can; and finally there was butchering time in the fall. But with all these out of the way and with longer, cooler nights came patchin' and darnin' time. Most of the patchin' at our house was done by the light of an old kerosene lamp. When the evening chores were finished, the table cleared, and the dishes washed, Mom would get her thimble, needle and thread and some patchin', then sit down to "rest" and patch. Mom's hands were chubby, nimble, and loving. I had watched those nimble fingers work the needle through the cloth. I had watched them string beans, hull fresh garden peas, work the milk out and salt into the fresh homemade butter, and knead the light bread. I had felt

62

The same nimble fingers quilted, patched and darned, just as they peeled pie apples.

their healing touch on my fevered brow many times. I had also felt those hands on the seat of my overalls for doing wrong, yet not one time did I ever doubt that she loved me. She had a way of telling me, but a better way of showing me.

Mom liked to build "air castles" ... so while she patched or darned, we visited and built air castles. Sometimes when she was patching patches, as she often did, her air castles seemed subdued. Or when a draft on the old floor sifted snow into little drifts near the kitchen door, it sorta chilled her faith a little, but she would cover the waver with the word *someday*. We would always do it someday. We had moved from a one-room native oak cabin to a tiny four-room board and batten house made of rough oak with two unfinished rooms upstairs and two rooms downstairs with a connecting ladder and a clapboard-covered roof. This, of course, was some progress, but it still took a lot of faith and imagination to see ourselves living in a beautiful white cottage with pretty wallpaper and carpets and china and curtains and furniture and screen doors and screened windows, but the way she described it, it surely would be "something" and we would have it "someday."

In those days the thimble, needle, and thread were

more important to survival than the artist's brush or the poet's pen. But the yearning for beauty and hunger for the finer things were ever present. So Mom's spirits soared rapidly and her air castles became more elegant, elaborate, and vivid when she began to plan a new quilt.

The patchwork quilt was a product of long winter nights . . . a blend of thrift, imagination, and hundreds of hours of tireless work culminating in a thing of beauty. Often they were too pretty to use. Many were folded and saved for wedding gifts, and so they became heirlooms. Sure enough, when Evelyn and I were married, Mom gave us "The Wedding," "Ocean Wave," and "Joseph's Coat of Many Colors." And now, after 38 years, "Joseph's Coat" is on the bed of our oldest grandson, Ken Webster.

Mom saved every scrap of cloth from making aprons, dresses, and shirts. She searched the *Kansas City Star*, the *St. Louis Globe Democrat*, and the *Capper's Farmer* for quilt patterns. The smaller the pieces of the design the more valuable the quilt. She would spend hundreds of hours sewing the tiny pieces together into neat blocks, all by hand with thimble and needle and thread, and finally the blocks into a quilt top.

Mom always had mixed emotions when she started to put the quilt into the frame. Dad always complained because it took up most of one room, but when the muslin was stretched, the cotton batting was spread in place, and the brand new quilt top was laid in place, she could see how beautiful it would look and that would be her reward.

. . . Much quilting was done in quilting bees. The besetting sin of most quilting bees was gossip. So when the neighbor ladies were invited to help quilt, they made sure they were there . . . if for no other reason than self-defense.

THE STAFF OF LIFE

That warm autumn Sunday evening I was going back, going back to the home of my boyhood, a rocky 4-acre hillside farm, a land once upon a time covered with big virgin timber, underbrush, wild briars, and grape vines.

The paint brushes of autumn, quickened by an early frost, were changing the green oak leaves of last summer to tired rusty browns, a contrast to the bright yellow leaves of the hickorys. The shumate, sassafras, and dogwood were dabbing their brilliant reds and maroons into harmonious profusion on the canvas of nature. One could hear the rustling leaves as they rasped against one another in a gentle breeze; soon the leaves would fall to a damp earth to be no more.

Recollecting is curious; as I turned left off the blacktop to follow a winding gravel road along the river, landmarks—visible and invisible—began to assert themselves upon my memory. The Gum Springs Missionary Baptist Church, organized in 1896, an old-style frame building still sitting upon a leveled-off hillside, its name derived from a big spring bubbling from an old gum tree stump, had helped to change the lives and destinies of many wayward folks. And the spring had quenched the thirst of hundreds of weary travelers. It was here I first attended church and Sunday school.

The Bud Myers' place at the fork of the road was still a well-kept farm—run by the same family for nearly 100 years. Then Mason School, nothing left but a rusty pump in a pasture, but my memory served me well. I could still see all 17 kids, the big wood stove, the loose bark shattered on the floor, the blackboard, the pictures of Columbus and Washington hanging behind the teacher's crude desk. I could feel the painful stobs, stubble and briars under my bare feet that the mower had left when it cut a summer's growth off the playground. That year we had had money enough for a five-month term. . . . Now the last turn up the dim, dusty lane. The dense growth of underbrush formed a cool, shadowy tunnel over the lane. Blackberry and huckleberry vines were still growing along the edge of the lane. I had picked blackberries right here and carried them home in a bucket for Mom to make jelly. I could still feel the salty sweat burning in the fresh briar scratches on my arms. I could still feel the fine, soft dust oozing up between my bare toes; I could see the tracks of field mice, terrapin, and fox in the fine dust where they crossed the lane.

My heart sank. The homeplace was gone. Gone were the old box house and the barn—without a trace. I climbed through the sagging three-barbed wire fence to look around. I so hoped I could find something I could tie to my boyhood. A few flat rocks may have been part of the piers the house sat on . . . a light shallow dip in the soil where the cellar used to be . . . a spot where I thought the well was located. I kicked the soil around where I thought Dad's blacksmith shop had been: four 10-foot posts set in the ground with an improvised

10 x 14 foot tin roof attached to the side of the smoke-house and covering a dirt floor. It was more shade than shelter. Dad's blacksmith tools had been crude, but essential . . . a hand-turned forge and anvil, several hammers for various purposes, chisels and tongs, a tempering tub, an 18-inch grinding stone about 2½ inches thick mounted in two notches on an improvised wooden stand with a peddle on each side and a cross board to sit on, a tin can with a small hole in the bottom tied to a wire hanging from the roof. When filled with water, it would drip on the stone and keep it wet while Dad was grinding. Rocky soil and tree roots were hard on plow points. So Dad had used every rainy day and sometimes noon hours heating and hammering out plow points, shoeing horses, filing saws, grinding axes, scythes and cradles. I had learned a little about heating, shaping, and tempering steel as I watched and helped Dad work.

The garden was gone, too. But I could still see the weedless rows of big-headed cabbage, the lettuce beds, the radishes, the yellow crook-necked squash, the slim green onions, the long rows of green beans, the gooseberry bushes, currant bushes, and the pungent sage Mom used in making sausage in the fall and in turkey dressing at Thanksgiving and Christmas time.

The two acres Dad had first cleared and planted in strawberries were now covered with second growth timber. Some of the red oak was over two feet in diameter. The second year Dad had cleared two more acres and set out a small orchard—a variety of apples, peaches, plums, and cherries—then made elaborate plans for our first wheat crop. That fall Dad sowed winter wheat in the young orchard to make good use of the land while the young trees were growing. Dad anticipated a big yield of wheat. As it turned out there was more expectation than yield. Mom declared the wheat that would go to Gaither's watermill to be the "staff of life." In her old cast iron stove, she would convert that flour to light thick-crusted bread and biscuits. The balance would be shared with Mom's Rhode Island Red hens, two pigs, Maude the cow, and Molly and May, our horses.

In February, we had moved into the big league. Dad bought May, a seven-year-old white mare with small, dark brown specks all over her. Dad described her as a "flea-bitten gray." She was hard-headed, tough-mouthed, uncouth, rawboned, and slow. Molly was a dapple-gray, smooth as a peeled onion, spirited and ladylike. It made little difference what we did or how we did it, May was always behind . . . a trial of one's patience.

A mild winter, a warm spring sun and generous showers urged the wheat to do its best. By harvest time the wheat was about shoulder high to me—a billowing sea of golden-bearded heads. For the most part, the cradle or scythe was before my time. We were now entering the binder age, and most of the river farmers had them. Our wheat was about ready, but we couldn't afford to hire a binder. Anyway three horses and binder would be too large to get around our small fruit trees. So Dad would cradle the wheat. Each sweep of the cradle would cut a swath about two feet wide and five or six feet long in a slight circle. He would drop each sweep in a loose bundle in a neat row. Dad taught me how to gather several sweeps, tie them with binding twine, shock several of the bundles together and carefully cover with a "cap sheath." If I did it right, only the grain in the cap sheath would get wet in a rain and would dry out quickly when the sun shone. When the wheat was cut and shocked in neat rows, Dad and Mom liked the way it looked; it made them feel sorta like they were wheat farmers.

The threshing season involved all the farmers for several miles up and down the river and lasted for four to six weeks. For the most part the work was traded and required some attention in keeping track of time and engaging the threshing machine and scheduling the farmers. Not many dollars changed hands, but a lot of labor did. The threshing circle usually began with the last farmer last year. He would be the first this year and so on. This year Pete Alley would be the first. Threshing required about 25 men and eight to ten bundle wagons and teams, and that would be next Tuesday. Three or four teams and wagons with grain-tight boxes were needed to haul from the separator. Sometimes the grain was sacked in burlap sacks in the field for easier handling.

Cooking for a threshing crew of 25 or so every dinner and supper—sometimes six days a week for four to six weeks—represented hard work and lots of it as well as organization. Just about every housewife in the neighborhood had a part in it.

Our grain crop was too small for a set. So Monday evening we took three loads of our bundles down the hill to Pete Alley's. Ours would be the first to thresh while the dew was drying off the fields.

The threshing outfit was there setting up the biggest machine I had ever been close to. The red separator was sitting almost north and south with the blower pipe a little toward the northeast. A prevailing southwest wind would blow the chaff and straw from the machine. The big Frick steam tractor was spewing, hissing, and chugging, getting lined up about a hundred feet from the separator, a thick eight-inch belt with one twist was on the big pulleys being tightened. A big pile of old post and fence rails would be used for fuel; a span of mules and the water boy were bringing in the water wagon. Those old fence posts and rails would convert that load of water to hundreds of horsepower of steam tomorrow. My teeth chattered with excitement. It was said this outfit could thresh 1500 to 2000 bushels of well-headed wheat a day. That meant our crop would last about 15 minutes. If the truth had been known, threshing our crop was at best an accommodation and maybe a nuisance. Dad dropped a bundle of 50 patched burlap sacks on the ground near the elevator side of the separator, and we went home.

A hot July sun was peeping over the treetops when we hit the floor the next morning. Dad said it would burn the dew off by eight o'clock. We were at Pete Alley's at seven. Most of the crew was there, too. The big Frick steam engine was belching smoke and throbbing with power. The fire in the firebox was white hot and roaring and making white clouds in the damp morning air. The separator man with a big, long-spouted oil can in his gloved hand was giving the machine last minute attention. Dad with our bundle wagon drove Molly and May up to the feeder. Molly had never been that close to anything that looked that big and dangerous before. I knew a loud or sudden noise would cause her to come unglued. We hadn't had May long enough to know how she would behave, but as a caution, two of the men got a hold of their bridles and began talking to them and rubbing their necks and manes while Dad kept the lines in his hands. All of a sudden the whistle blew; then the engineer began to open the throttle; the belt began to move, and the huge red monster became alive.

Dad tossed the first bundle of our own wheat on the feeder table. Almost instantly a golden stream of Mom's creamy brown "staff of life" began pouring into the patched burlap sacks. A few seconds later the big blower sent clouds of straw and chaff through the straw pipe into our strawpile. Threshing at the rate of 250 bushels of wheat an hour, it didn't take long to get our two acres through the machine and our 47 bushels of wheat in our sacks. Our neighbors told Dad 24 bushels per acre was good on upland. Dad paid 7¢ per bushel—$3.29.

The separator man turned the blower pipe a different direction and started on Pete Alley's wheat. After paying all the help back, Dad worked the balance of the threshing season helping—for $1.50 a day and his dinner.

Eating threshing crew dinners was like eating Sunday dinners six times a week. Just about any man in the crew, including me, could get by on a half pound of meat for dinner or supper if there were at least two helpings of mashed potatoes and gravy, green beans, homemade bread and butter, wilted lettuce, green onions, a piece of a 9- or 10-inch pie cut in four pieces and (not or) a chunk of waxie devil's food cake and choice of coffee, cold tea (we didn't have ice), sweet milk, or buttermilk. To feed a threshing crew in those days, you started the day before by chasing down 6 or 8 long yellow-legged chickens, slicing a country ham, picking and snapping two or three gallons of green beans, washing a half-bushel of leaf lettuce, pulling and skinning green onions. The morning started at five o'clock with the baking of nine or ten apple and cherry pies . . . and frying chickens and sliced ham . . . baking a couple of shallow bread pans filled with a waxie devil's food cake to be smeared with a thick layer of rich creamy chocolate icing. It took some good cooks who were willing to work and sweat to serve up that kind of eating at five minutes past twelve six days a week for four or five weeks. Mom helped almost every day just to be a good neighbor. I made my services available at no charge. The last day we threshed, the engineer told me personally that I was an expert at blowing the whistle and carrying drinking water to the crew, that I was the best steam gauge and water glass watcher that he ever had. He said he'd bet a pocket knife that I would own my own steam engine and threshing machine someday. And I believed every word he said . . . though I never was equal to the prediction.

The sun was low in the west and its red rays were enhancing the autumn scenes as I climbed back through the sagging wire fence. As I drove home in the remaining moments of twilight I asked myself whether the old homestead had changed? . . . Not really . . . I had felt the warmth and affection of my mother, I had sensed the determination of my dad, I had recognized the pride of their achievements. They had taught me by word and deed that if I pressed the limits, I would be what I could be.

THE GUNNY SACK

The gunny sack, also known as burlap, was as much a part of early American farm life as horse collars, turning plows, milk crocks, butter churns and cast iron cookstoves. It was packaging at its very best . . . would hold anything but water . . . and at least a hundred pounds of it. The sacks usually smelled like whatever was in them, but the contents never smelled like the sack. The empty sacks always smelled the same except when they were wet; then they smelled "surenuff" awful. They were used for everything . . . usually printed in bright colors with trademarks, pictures of livestock or the products they contained. It was as impossible to operate a small farm without gunny sacks as it was without rain.

Where we lived, mountain land, was better suited for small fruits, apples, and peaches, so we expected to run out of stock feed and finish each winter season buying grain by the sack. Dad, kidding, said he hoped to sell enough empty sacks to pay the mortgage off . . . but Mom always beat him to them. Mom was by gunny sacks like some ladies are with trading stamps . . . she saved them. They were worth about two cents each, the patched ones a little less. She was always saving sacks to get a luxury item, say, bright oil cloth for the kitchen table, curtains for the front room or a bedspread. It took a long time to get enough together, but with a strong imagination she could anticipate how the new item would look a long time before she got it.

Among the men folks, the gunny sack was a status symbol at the threshing machine, bean huller, or potato shed. Rivalry in sack sewing by hand was serious . . . the speed with which you could sew a full sack and produce a good ear on each side for hand-holds would not only give you a great deal of recognition but guarantee a job for a whole season.

In those days the men were separated from the boys the day they could shoulder a hundred pound "sack o' something" and "heist" it over the edge of a wagon box. And when you could do it all day, you had moved over into a man's world and everybody, including the girls, would admire you for it. Of course, this posed a nutritional problem; it took more than three-fourths ounce of cereal and a glass of skim milk to last a half day. You needed ham and eggs and biscuits and butter and lots of whole milk straight from the cow. At noon it was fried chicken, the kind that weighed four or five pounds on foot . . . with well-developed legs (that had been busy chasing grasshoppers), potatoes and gravy and pie and—not or—cake.

At night it was the same thing over. The food didn't have time to turn into fat or cholesterol: it was burned up in six hours. It did well to last a half day.

There wasn't any room to get into trouble either. When you took a bath, you not only washed off the dirt, but dried salty sweat, sometimes more sweat than dirt! You went to bed, not with mental fatigue, but with every muscle and every bone weary from real toil. You went to

Gunny sacks were worth 2¢ apiece, patched ones a little bit less.

bed without feeling you had been abused or deprived and to sleep without sedatives. You slept like a log and awoke to a new day without depression, excited and thankful that the door of opportunity had been left open. The world was out there and you were convinced you could conquer your part of it.

The year I was six years old I got acquainted with another way to use a gunny sack. This was the year I started to school and, as usual, there was a cash problem—not enough to buy new overalls, shirts, books, and all the other things essential to "edgicate" a boy. So some Rhode Island Red hens that weren't laying had to span the gap. Mom had a system for checking up on an old hen's egg-laying ability . . . by up-ending her. If Mom could get three fingers between the hen's pelvic bones, that hen escaped the trip to town; if Mom could only get two fingers between the pelvic bones, the old hen was a goner and into the gunny sack she would go. Mom checked out 35 to 40 hens before she found 10 hens whose egg-laying potential was questionable. They would have a value of about 50¢ each.

When Dad loaded the gunny sacks and the hens into the boot of the buggy, he discovered that the hot August sun would soon take its toll if the old hens didn't get some air. He cut holes in the sacks; then, with their heads run through the holes, they made their way to town with beaks gapping, panting for dear life.

The spring before the summer I was eight I discovered another use for a gunny sack. Dad paid a neighbor $2 a piece for 3 pigs that weighed about 35 pounds each; they

The aroma of fresh cured hay was always welcome
because it meant that the cows, horses and mules
would eat throughout the winter.

were to be our next winter's meat. The price was F.O.B. the neighbors. So it was my job to get them home. Here I made another discovery: a pig's head is always on the wrong end and his feet always pointed in the wrong direction to go into a gunny sack. And it is not easy to tie a sack securely when a pig is determined to get out while you are doing it. I also discovered that the squeal of an unhappy pig could not be muffled by a gunny sack and the farther you carried him the louder it seemed to get.

I was just a little feller, too, when I discovered that a cane pole, cork, hook, line, and sinker combined with a gunny sack made fishing gear that was unequalled. The folks that lived in the only house between us and the creek were good fishermen. Since I rarely caught anything big enough to show off, the wet gunny sack concealed my embarrassment when I passed their house on the way home.

Of all the ways to use a gunny sack that I remember, I believe I cherish the memories of homemade ice cream best of all. It all started four miles from home—in town—when we put a big block of ice in a gunny sack, wrapped it in an old quilt and headed for home. With boyish anticipation I could hardly wait. The minute we arrived home I grabbed a milk bucket and started to hunt old Maud, our family cow. Of all the cows we had, I loved her best. She had long teats, was easy to milk; she would milk from either side, with or without feed . . . any place . . . anytime . . . and never moved a foot. She was good for 2 gallons of rich yellow milk twice a day. (The sounds of the first streams of milk spraying on the bottom of the milk bucket are unforgettable. As the spraying sounds are muffled by the rising foam, you are overwhelmed by a sense of tranquility and well-being. You are as close to nature as you will ever be.) On ice cream night, my thoughts were on my empty stomach and the better things to come. By the time I got the milk to the house, Mom had gathered the eggs and Dad had beaten the ice to a pulp with the broad side of a double-bitted axe; the gunny sack was beaten so full of holes it would barely hold the ice. Mom was ridiculously clean by the standards of her day; she strained the milk through two thicknesses of a 10-pound cloth sugar sack. About all she got out of it was straw and trash, but it looked clean and tasted fine. It's amazing what can happen to fresh eggs, vanilla extract, and whole milk straight from the cow when it is put in an old ice cream freezer and surrounded with beaten-up ice and salt and turned as long as you could last. I know one thing: if you ate the results too fast, you would have a headache.

THE COUNTY FAIR

Many of you will recall that the grocery store or supermarket of childhood days was a large garden spot and about 1½ acres of truck patches that always included nearly all of the many berries and fruits, radishes, lettuce, onions, cabbage, potatoes, sweet corn, popcorn, pumpkins, squash, beans, melons, cucumbers, peanuts, etc.

You were taught the art and science of converting fertile seed, rainfall, good soil, and tender care into lush fruit and vegetables for the table and cellar. You didn't need a store much.

The life of our rural ancestors was a self-sufficient one. They needed little from anyone or anything outside of their own homestead. They battled the frost and drought, floods and insects; when they won, the victory was sweet, and they canned, cured, preserved and dried the yield. If they lost, they kept their dignity, for they had lost to a respected enemy. During times of victory, the best of many things was taken to the County Fair. The

County Fair provided an opportunity to show the talents and resourcefulness of the home and farm.

Home canning and preserving were taken seriously in those days and considerable local fame could be gained from a delicacy that had unusual taste and appearance. The exhibits of hundreds of jars of canned fruit, jellies and preserves, vegetables, and pickles and relishes reflected the individuality of ladies throughout the county. Here and there a blue ribbon had to be reward enough because there was little, if any, prize money to win.

The livestock exhibits were simple . . . just good, sound animals that were well brushed, combed, and braided, whose pedigree was unknown and unimportant, but whose good disposition or good looks had won them a place in the hearts of the family.

It was the big crowds, the noisy music, bright-colored stands and the home canning department, in that order, that I remember best about the County Fairs when I was a kid.

"Goodie . . . Goodie . . . Goodie . . . out of the old town pump . . . all you can drink for a nickel," sang the barker and that is exactly what I did . . . with unfortunate results. It was 1922, my first County Fair, and I had a quarter to blow in only three days. So that ice-cold red lemonade pouring out of that pitcher pump looked good . . . especially to a country kid who had drunk ordinary well water all summer.

Now that the red lemonade had lowered my assets by

The old car ferry

20%, I decided it might be wise to look around a little before I plunged into some other extravagance. My original plan was to be cautious the first two days, save back about 15¢, and then really live it up the last day. With 20¢ jingling in my pocket, I strolled, bug-eyed and wide-mouthed, through the crowd.

The Merry-Go-Round was quite a machine. I especially liked the steam part . . . listening to the steam hiss in the engine . . . and the way that black coal smoke belched out of the boiler. I didn't care much about the horses though; we had them at home. But the steam "kelleo" (calliope) and its music really were something . . . and business, boy! I decided right there, that was my kind of business.

The doll rack looked like a good proposition at 3 balls for a nickel; you got all you knocked off. I knew I was pretty good with a rock, so the price was the only thing that kept me from making a killing.

I passed a tent with a high platform in front . . . a gang of ladies were performing. A big, important man referred to them as beauties, said they were going to put on

81

a big show. I didn't remember seeing them in church or Sunday school.

The fairground was filled with equally important things to see and eat, and I spent the day investigating every proposition; in the end though it was a wad of cotton candy about the size of a football that looked the nearest like a nickel's worth and I plunked down my second nickel for the day.

Friday held great promise: a free ballgame and an aeroplane with a wing-walker. This would be the first time most folks, including me, had ever seen a plane, and I could hardly wait for the next day. As I recall, Friday morning was clear and warmed by a mid-September sun. Our buggy was neither the first nor the only one on the way to the fair.

A large grove separated the fairgrounds and the field where they played ball. The grove was a shady place, and here the horses were usually tied to the trees; so today it would be filled with horses, buggies, surreys, and wagons.

As I remember, we visited the women's building in the morning. I soon discovered that those long lines of Mason fruit jars filled with every sort of preserved food could certainly whet a hungry boy's appetite. It was right here that I found another business that I would like to be in—the fair-judging business; I would get to taste nearly everything in that business. Besides the canned food, the building was filled with cakes, bread, pies, cookies, and bonnets, quilts, comforters, rugs, and dresses.

The big moment was nearing . . . almost dinnertime. We had cold fried chicken and potato salad in the boot of the buggy. I had secret hopes that Dad would let me wash it down with a bottle of "sodie pop."

The ballgame was well underway. I don't remember now who was playing because out of the north appeared an aeroplane, a huge yellow thing with two wings and one engine in the middle. A fellow was standing on the right wing holding to a wire with one hand and waving with the other. The next time the plane came around, it suddenly shot upward and over in what some called a "loop." How that fellow stayed on that wing was a mystery to me. In a few minutes the plane returned. This time the man was hanging by his toes from the axle of the plane. Some people said, "The fool will kill himself." On the return trip, the plane was much higher than on previous trips. It looked like the man was hanging from the axle by his heels when suddenly he slipped and his body came tumbling through the air. The women screamed and covered their faces with their handkerchiefs. Men gasped, and kids froze with fright. A soft breeze caused the body to drift a little and it came tumbling down through the trees in the edge of the grove. The crash and the noise scared a lot of horses . . . caused them to break loose; a lot of harnesses, buggies, and wagons were damaged by the runaway horses. Nearly everybody that wasn't grief stricken rushed to the scene of the tragedy . . . to discover a dummy.

*The sabbath was sacred, a reflection of the farm
family's culture, tradition and sense of place.*

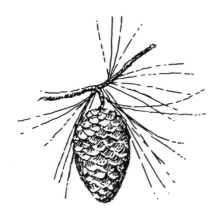

THE BASKET

The horse and buggy, distance, and bad roads sheltered the old-time farmer from the shock of instant news. Most news traveled via the drummer (salesman) to the village store and from there to the farmer and was history by at least thirty days before he knew anything about it. And most "news" happened so far away that it made little difference if it was good or bad. The farmer's world was the township or at most the county. The largest town he knew about was the county seat. It was on this island of isolation that he became self-sufficient and fiercely independent. Most folks he knew were farmers too and produced about the same crops; so his market was limited and cash was non-existent. Therefore, what he needed was home-grown or home-made—or he did without.

In his world of drought, flood, wind, hail, weeds, and insects, the hoe or axe was more functional than the artist's brush. The needle, thimble, and thread were more important to survival than the poet's pen. But the yearning for beauty draws no line: the hunger for the finer things is ever present. So, as life seemed to get a little easier and there was more time, the things he shaped and designed—his house, his buggy, furniture, stoves, quilts, tools, pictures, weather vane, or his front gate—reflected his cultural and artistic taste and his rising affluence.

The early farmer's table was supported by his field, orchard, and garden via the smokehouse, cellar, pantry, and a big cast iron cookstove. The home was the cultural and entertainment center. Self-respect and discipline were homemade, too . . . sometimes taught on the seat of the pants by compassionate authority. Fun was homemade also . . . candy making, house parties, family singing around the old pump organ.

As the industrial age spread its influence and expanded its products to include rural and farm life, a new word was coined: *boughtin'* . . . boughtin' bread, boughtin' plows, boughtin' clothes, boughtin' seed, boughtin' haircuts, boughtin' everything.

The farmer finally traded his aching back and calloused hands for gasoline engines and electric power, his horses and hand-guided plows for bright tractors and flat tires. He swapped his peace and tranquility for instant news, market reports, boughtin' entertainment— and ulcers and tensions. His barter system gave way to cash and credit. He was no longer in charge of his own security and destiny. He was now a member of the world society.

Today what is left of his relics, his pictures, his shapes and designs is held in high esteem and referred to as "folk art" and "antiques." And there is great effort to establish date and place of origin.

The basket and family orchard played an important role in this era. Baskets, like gunny sacks, were the containers for everything. In the mountains where white oak was available, basket-making was an art. Small white

86

Picking green beans kept a fellow out of trouble.

oak trees were cut when the sap was just right and the log split in several pieces, then placed on an improvised rack where the splints and stays were peeled or shaved off with what carpenters and cabinet makers called a draw knife. On occasion some of the stays and splints were dyed red or green and woven into the plain stays giving them decorative designs. There was a size or purpose for every basket and names like egg basket, picnic basket, clothes basket, pie basket, and grocery basket suggested their uses. There were several shapes too. The hardest to make were the gizzard baskets (shaped a little like a chicken gizzard). The hand-woven basket has always evaded automation and is a dying art, today restricted to a relatively few mountain people.

As farms grew larger and fewer and the rural people migrated toward the manufacturing centers, markets for the farmer's produce began to develop. The "packaging" age was born. Machinery was developed to make high production baskets shaped sorta like the ceramic basket, but made from wood and wire.

In the beginning the baskets were of two sizes . . . bushel and half-bushel. Eventually most crops were priced and sold in one-bushel units. Fruit and potatoes were especially adapted to the new form of marketing. Baskets with contrasting colors and attractive trim were made to enhance buyer appeal. A method that is hard to explain was developed to fill the top of the basket first. The fruit was placed into a neat ring or other design known as "ringing" or "facing them filled." When the basket was turned right side up again it had a beautiful design and a smooth appearance; the only trouble was sometimes the best fruit was the facing fruit.

I am sure Dad and Mom had a Johnny Appleseed point of view when they traded our 40-acre rocky hillside farm that was split right down the middle east and west with a deep ravine and a big spring for 35 acres of almost rockless upland that had second-growth sprouts, sage grass, and a $500 mortgage. Dad and Mom were armed with a will to work, the assurance of the Lord's help, an undaunted faith in the future and "air castles" unlimited. Somehow I think they envisioned a time when they would be known as Mr. and Mrs. James Daniel Webster, the rich fruit people.

For the next two years we survived on hard work, faith, and air castles. We grubbed sprouts, burned sage grass, plowed and planted 14 of the 35 acres in orchard. I became the official "brush burner." Dad said I was one of the best he had known . . . I liked to have killed myself trying to live up to his expectations.

The fall and winter after we set the orchard was cold and severe. We fought cottontail rabbits all winter trying to keep them from eating the tender bark of the young trees. We made paper tubes by wrapping newspaper around a broom handle and tying them with string, then sliding them down and over the young tender switches. This worked until the big snow came and the rabbits could reach above the paper tubes. Some of the trees bore the rabbit scars until I was grown.

Dad and Mom became well known as the "fruit people." They were admired for their hard work and thrift—but never known as rich.

Years later—it seemed like an eternity—my dad plunked down $3.60 for three dozen bushel baskets and lids with a green band around the top and middle. He faced and packed 30 bushels, all there were, of fancy eating apples of three varieties: Jonathan, Staymen Winesaps, and Red Delicious. The rest of the crop was faulty and went to the vinegar plant or the apple evaporator and was sliced for dried apples. I think Dad and Mom realized for the first time that late freezes, drought, hail, and insects would prevent them from becoming rich fruit people.

Two dogs and a good straw hat: that's happiness!

MR. RICE'S COFFEE MILL

One of my strongest childhood impressions was Mr. Rice's coffee house. I remember Mr. Rice got his coffee in large bags which probably weighed over 100 pounds. They had the names of coffee plantations and towns in Central and South America printed in big black letters. I used to stare at a name and wonder how that faraway country looked . . . wishing that I could visit there someday when I grew up.

(Many years later I did visit the coffee-producing areas of Guatemala, Costa Rica, Honduras, El Salvador, Colombia, Equador, and Peru. Coffee is indeed a great and profitable crop for growers and provides employ-ment for thousands of people. The beans are gathered from the shrub-like trees and spread out two to six inches deep on the flat ground or concrete slab to dry under a blazing hot tropical sun. Then they are turned over about every day by bare-backed Indian and Spanish people with large scoop shovels. When they are dry, they are scooped into large burlap-type bags to be shipped by ocean-going freighters to a coffee thirsty world.)

Well, it was a long way to haul coffee, but Mr. Rice got a shipment with some degree of regularity, and Saturday was the big day. The minute we got to town, we could smell coffee roasting at Mr. Rice's. There's no telling how many tons of coffee he sold on the basis of smell alone. Most of the coffee was sold in berry form in those days; so it was sacked in brown kraft bags as it came from the ancient roaster. Mr. Rice had a way of wrapping the string around the bag and flipping a bow knot so quickly that I never quite caught on how he did it.

Folks would grind coffee at home when they needed it in an old wooden coffee mill. It was believed the coffee would keep its "strength" longer by grinding it as needed. Mr. Rice had a big old red coffee mill just in case someone didn't have his own. The mill was mounted on a heavy cast iron base that was bolted to the floor. The hopper was the size of a water bucket. A bright metal scoop was directly under the mill and hopper to catch the ground coffee. Two red 20-inch, cast iron wheels with wooden handles and the manufacturer's name cast right into the metal, and one was slipped on a shaft on each side of the hopper. On many occasions Mr. Rice asked me to crank the mill for him. I had to stand on my tiptoes to do so, but I was delighted to help—especially if there were several on hand to watch me.

But one Saturday we discovered a "tragic" thing had happened. Right in the middle of the store sat a huge machine—a coffee mill—bright red, trimmed in gold, with a shiny hopper on each side and a big scoop under each hopper and, of all things, an electric motor. It was plain to see Mr. Rice expected his coffee business to grow. Now he could serve two customers at a time. The new mill would grind twice as fast as the old one. All told he could serve the people four times as fast.

Mr. Rice's coffee house continued to fill the streets with the same fragrant aroma of fresh-roasted coffee. Mr. Rice continued to greet his customers with the same affectionate voice and smile, but I was out of the coffee-grinding business.

Many years later the bright lithographed vacuum can filled with big name ground coffee began to make its appearance, and Mr. Rice bowed out to progress.

Strawberry pickers waiting for the dew to dry

MOM'S NEW RANGE

"We will buy a new range . . . if we have a good fruit crop." It was the third year in a row that Dad had promised the new stove.

Our hopes were dashed to dust the first year by drought: no rain to speak of from early April 'til June 1st. Strawberries and blackberries were small, seedy, and unsaleable; worms ate the peaches; apples were so small they went to the vinegar plant.

The following year our hopes were high until what Dad called "a late Easter squall" moved in: a day of lightning and thunder and torrents of rain followed by clearing skies and a bone-chilling northwest wind. That night we watched the thermometer tumble below the 32 degree mark and slide on down to 19 degrees before a warm morning sun came to the rescue . . . too late. Gone were an acre and a half of peaches, 12 acres of apples, a big patch of blackberries and 3 acres of strawberries. Gone, too, were all the work, plans, and air castles for another year.

The frontier spirit in Dad and Mom soon gave birth to new attitudes, hopes, and determination. Mom mentioned it might be the Lord's way to keep us humble, and sure enough it did. You don't have any trouble staying humble when you have to look to a flock of old hens and a few milk cows for survival.

The kitchen was a small lean-to arrangement attached to a four-room house (two room upstairs and two down with a connecting ladder). The lean-to had been built during a more prosperous time when more room was thought to be needed. A heavy drab paper (known then as oatmeal paper) was tacked to the wall with tacks that had been run through small squares of cardboard.

Mom's cookstove was a small, almost square, four-holed, black stove sitting on four skinny legs, with a protruding hearth and draft in front, and a tiny oven with doors on each side. The six-inch stovepipe went straight through the sloping roof. When it rained, water would nearly always run down the stove pipe into the stove . . . unless it was hot . . . then the water would turn to steam. The cookstove was backed against the north wall; a dilapidated wood box was on the left; a rickety, oil-cloth-covered table was on the right and just under a half window. A cabinet with perforated metal panels in the doors and sides (sometimes referred to as a "pie safe") was against the opposite wall. A "built-in" cupboard about 2½ feet square was just to the right of the living room door. A split-printed curtain hid the Mason jars of canned fruit, vegetables and preserves from sight. A galvanized water bucket, a tin wash pan and a bar of homemade lye soap were supported by a three-cornered shelf just to the left of the outside door. The outside wall leaned in a little, and the back door sagged enough to wear a perfect circle in the bare floor. It wasn't at all difficult to stay humble.

"Come here, Jim!" It was the distress in Mom's voice that caused Dad and me to rush to her aid. With tears of despair streaming down her cheeks, she pointed at two chocolate pies she had just removed from the oven. The meringue and crust were burned black on the side of one; both were covered with wood ashes and soot. It was plain to see the old oven was a goner so far as baking was concerned. So there on the spot, for the third time, Dad promised, "We will buy a new range . . . if we have a good fruit crop."

If small fruit, strawberries and blackberries, could survive all of the hazards of nature, they could solve most of our financial woes and determine our future plans—a new range in this case—because they were the first cash crop in the spring and early summer.

It was the first of April when Dad's promise gave rebirth to Mom's faith and hope. This spring held great promise: warm days and gentle showers began to arrive early. It was only six weeks or so until strawberries would be ripe.

Mom ordered every cookstove catalogue in the country; she studied mail order catalogues for wallpaper styles and linoleum designs . . .

We lived in constant fear of frost and drought. If the sun shone all day, we thought sure it was the beginning of a drought. If it rained or the wind changed, we just knew it would freeze or frost before morning, but as each day went by, the prospect of frost diminished; finally only drought or hail could alter our plans.

The first few days of May were warm and humid. We were visited by warm spring showers almost every night. The strawberry plants were loaded with blooms and maturing berries. Dad found the first ripe berry May 7th. I was dispatched to tell the neighbors, who had promised to help. We would pick Monday, May 10.

The first picking yielded ten 24-quart crates, flushed a dozen cotton-tail rabbits and revealed four bob-white quail nests with eggs. Twenty-two dollars and fifty cents was a lot of money for 10 crates of berries and the biggest fist full of money Dad had had in a long time. The buyers said it had been a long time since the people had all the fresh strawberries they could eat. The chances were good that the price would stay strong . . . and it did. By May 20 the strawberry crop had come and gone and we had enough money to pay the pickers, the crates, the interest, taxes, some overdue cow feed bills and buy a 100-pound sack of canning sugar . . . but not enough for a cookstove yet. Mom pointed out that the Lord knew her tithes were paid to date, so she pinned her faith to Malachi 3:10-11. Dad pinned his hopes on the showers and warm sunshine. I had been taught that it was hard to out-give the Lord, so my faith was tied to both. Now it was up to the Lord and the big blackberry patch to come through with Mom's new range.

For one week it didn't rain. Mom's faith held firm; mine wavered; Dad worried. After what seemed to be an eternity, it rained again and those big juicy berries began to ripen. It was decided, over my protest, that we wouldn't even eat berries with cream and sugar, nor would we can any until we had sold enough to get Mom's new range. We didn't eat any or can any that year, but we had enough money for Mom's range.

The first Saturday morning following the last berry pickin' found us on the road to town with Molly and May hitched to our old Webber wagon, Mom and Dad perched on the spring seat, Mom dressed in a bright red gingham dress, Dad in blue denim overalls, white shirt and tie; both wore a smile of triumph and victory. I stood barefooted behind the spring seat in a pair of scratchy pants.

Mom chose a light patterned wallpaper at Mr. Henry's Hardware, the paint and linoleum at the Benton County Hardware; but it was at Mr. Foss's hardware where a new range caught her eye and captured her heart. . . mine too. I didn't know anything could be that pretty: a cast iron range with a reservoir, warming closet doors, backsplash, a white porcelain oven door . . . with a built-in thermometer. It was the price that dampened our enthusiasm . . . $24.95 . . . a whole lot more than Mom had planned to pay. But it was love at first sight, and there was no recourse. Dad plunked down two tens and a five of hard-earned blackberry money and got a nickel back.

Mom's range was loaded into the wagon carefully. The 2½ joints of new stovepipe, linoleum, a gallon of paint and several rolls of wallpaper were rearranged to assure a safe ride over a jolty road home. It was a precious cargo as far as we were concerned.

Just before we left for home, Mr. Foss gave Mom a pretty white granite tea kettle as a gift. After that, Mom always thought you got more than you paid for at Mr. Foss's.

Molly and May couldn't understand all the rush to get home. Every time they slowed up, Dad would tap them with a whip. Mom insisted that we set the range up that evening. She would cook supper on it that very night. It was fun setting up the stove. I will never forget the first fire built in that range . . . how it smoked. It was the stove-black burning off, but it smelled new to me. Dad said the reservoir and tea kettle held over two buckets of water . . . that sounded like a lot when you had to draw it out of a dug well. That first night I nearly scalded my fingers testing the hot water in the reservoir.

Mom said she would get supper while Dad and I did the chores. It sure was hard to stay away from the house; Dad seemed in a hurry, too. Only half-way up the path from the barn, I could tell from the aroma in the air that Mom had cut a ham, and those slices would come right out of the middle tonight. The ham and gravy were just right for me, but the biscuits were almost black. Mom said she didn't understand the thermometer and declared that was the reason. At least they weren't covered with ashes and soot as they had been in the past.

When Mom asked the blessing on the food that night, she thanked the Lord for the stove too and gave him full credit for it . . . then asked him to help her to be a better cook, and somehow I always believed He did.

THE POT-BELLIED STOVE

It was 1919. The war was over and the boys were still coming home. The Kansas City Southern depot at Siloam Springs was like all other depots in the country: only a few months before it had been the scene of grief and heartbreak, but now almost every train brought a happy family reunion, the answer and the beginning of a new life.

The depot was relatively new, built of red brick with a red tile roof. A brick platform about 30 feet wide ran between the depot and the tracks for almost a block. It was the largest and prettiest building in town; we always pointed to it with pride.

Through some kind of communication, we had learned that several well known soldiers who had been prisoners of war "over there" would arrive Saturday night on the south-bound.

I know that my childhood memories are fragmentary and sometimes I have trouble getting them laid end-to-end in proper order, but in this instance I was too young for World War I to have any special significance. I had no idea where "over there" was except that it was a long way off. But I had heard the name "Kaiser Bill" many times, and it meant *bad.*

As I look back on this experience though, I can remember the air of expectancy as that special Saturday approached. Mom and Dad had discussed how the boys might look, how their sweethearts would act. Mom wondered if Mrs. McCollum would shout "Praise the Lord" or would just cry when Burton stepped off the train. I don't remember the date of this big Saturday but it was near Valentine's Day, a very cold, wet day; low hanging clouds were laden with sleet and rain. Dad put the side curtains on the buggy top, a storm curtain ran from the front bow down and over the dashboard. The storm curtain had a small yellow isinglass windshield and two slots for the reins to come through.

We were wrapped up head and ears; Molly struggled four miles in six-inch-deep mud trying to get us and the buggy through the dark to town. Even so, by the time we arrived, we were nearly frozen. Molly didn't know any more about a train than I did. It would be our first time to see one at night. Dad understood Molly's natural disposition well enough not to risk tying her too close to the tracks. A shrill whistle or a sudden hiss of escaping steam could be disastrous to the buggy . . . could even mean our walking home through the mud. So she was tied on the far side of the blacksmith shop and the livery stable . . . and we walked the last three blocks or so to the depot.

The swirling mist created halos around the dim yellow lights along the depot platform. A dozen steel-wheeled express wagons were lined up with the merchants' Saturday receipt of eggs, cream, cowhides and chickens. A few men and boys were sauntering around the platform. We soon discovered that other patriotic citizens were there to greet returning heroes, too. Horses hitched to buggies and wagons were tied everywhere.

The hum and chatter of happy voices greeted us as we entered the depot. The air had the strong sulphur odor of burning coal. I could see the blue smoke when I looked straight at the dingy lights. A big pot-bellied stove was doing its best to keep up with the falling temperature. It was red hot almost all the way around the bottom half. The draft door was wide open, and I could see the white hot clinkers and ashes as they fell through the grates. That old stove was sure busy that night. It was the biggest stove I had ever seen; this was the first coal I had watched burn and one of the few times I had ever smelled coal smoke—I sorta liked the smell—and it looked like an easier way to heat than cutting and hauling wood.

Until this night the only heating stove I knew anything about was a sheet-iron, wood-burning stove . . . generally known as a "King heater" . . . a "surenuff" poor people's stove. Even a little feller like me could easily see there was a big difference—although it was some later that I found out just how much fuel a big pot-bellied stove could burn in bad weather.

As I recall that Saturday night, the waiting room was warm and inviting . . . filled with grateful people. A ring of folks, mostly men, had their backs to the big stove soaking up the heat. I am sure there had been many anxious days and weeks since these folks were there to see their sons off to war, but tonight the atmosphere was light and cheerful. It wouldn't be long now. The big clock on the wall was ticking the seconds into minutes and minutes into train time. The black bulletin board under the clock said in crude chalk lettering "No. 9 ON TIME" . . . that meant about 8:30 p.m. Suddenly someone dashed through the door and announced they had heard the whistle. A stampede of uninhibited action followed. Soon folks were lined along the full depth of the platform. We could hear the low, throaty, almost mournful whistle long before the speeding train came around the curve into view. That monster, with clanging bell, came screeching by, not ten teet from where I stood, bringing a wake of tumbling paper and wet leaves. The whole platform was enveloped with a mixture of fog, steam, and coal smoke, the train finally stopping with the engine at the far end of the platform.

Since I wasn't interested in all the hugging and kissing, I decided to investigate the engine. I got to it just as the engineer was stepping down out of the cab. He had a big, long-spouted oil can in his gloved hand; he waved at me with the other and said, "Hi, Charlie" . . . I didn't know he called all boys Charlie. I was over-whelmed with the size of that throbbing giant . . . with the hissing and spewing of steam. With much authority, the engineer made his way around the engine oiling the places that needed oil. In a few minutes the bell began to ring again. The whistle tooted a few times, and the big engine jarred the earth as it began to leave.

Molly was cold and foxy . . . would hardly wait for Dad to untie her. As we came from behind the blacksmith shop, the depot was in full view. It was deserted now and would be until train time again.

After all the excitement of the returning soldiers, the trip home was a dreary contrast. Mom and Dad discussed the war, the soldiers, their sweethearts, the price of freedom and independence. Dad said, "The country would be better off if everybody had to pay the same price for their freedom and independence." I think Dad had the idea that wars were a poor man's fight and a rich man's profit. My thoughts were on the depot, the pot-bellied stove, and the train. I built some air castles that night. I was sure I could own a pot-bellied stove, a depot, and a railroad if I managed it right, but I went to bed that night with cold feet in a cold bed in a cold drafty house.

If you missed the pot-bellied stove and the era it represented, you have missed something. I am sure those who lived during that era will vouch for the truth of that statement.

Every farm boy could tell the age of a horse or a mule in the wagon days.

WAGON DAYS

The ruts in the muddy late November dirt road could barely be seen as Dad and I left for town with one rick of heating wood, a rick of finely split, dry oak cook wood, a handwoven basket full of Rhode Island Red hen eggs and a three-gallon can of hand-skimmed cream.

The wagon was heavy and hard to pull in the deep mud. The heavy burden caused the wheels to rumble and the hubs to clatter as they rolled over the rough, slushy road. The two white mares were well shod and the pressure of their weight and strength squirted the mud all over their white bellies and tails. The lower half of the old green Webber wagon box was splattered with mud. It was hard to tell the color of its bright red hubs and wheels. The cold northwest wind clawed at our hands and faces and flapped the old piece-quilt that was tucked around our legs. It was to be a memorable day for a boy of seven.

Dad was a respected man . . . but poor, enduring, and reliable. The load of wood was part of an agreement . . . a

107

payment on a doctor bill that was nearly a year old. Dr. Gullege had said he would take wood as he needed it; today he needed it. One more load and the bill would be paid.

Somehow as a boy I failed to see or feel anything wonderful or satisfying about wood cutting. To me it was a job, an unrewarding job of sawing a large tree close to the ground with a crosscut saw; the tree had been notched on one side with an axe to make it fall in the right direction. Then we trimmed all of the limbs and branches that were too small or short for a stick of wood and burned the brush on the spot.

Dad, being an ex-boy, sensed my view on wood cutting, so right there is where I first became an expert 'cause Dad said so. He said I was the best brush burner that he had ever seen . . . that if I did everything in life as well as I burned brush I would grow up to be big and important. (As it turned out, he was only half right . . . I grew up to be big.) It took a lot of Dad's bragging on my ability to burn brush to sustain a waning spirit and a growing hunger for a half-day at a time. (Dad's half-days were from daylight 'til twelve and one 'til dark.)

After I became an expert, turning green oak limbs into leaping yellow flames and fragrant blue smoke that drifted upward and onward into the blue forever had some virtue. Except for blistering my face and singeing my eyebrows and arms, I enjoyed watching the burning leaves float skyward. I watched and listened with curious eyes and ears as the yellow flames climbed along the burning limbs, sometimes spewing like a boiling tea kettle, sometimes popping like popcorn, consuming the strength of the wood, turning it into sparks, smoke and ashes . . . going back to that from which they came.

Just the thought or a plan to go to town on Saturday was the source of great joy and anticipation regardless of how you were to go, but when I was a boy, during early fall or winter the trip to town always included a load of wood at 75¢ to $1.50 a rick. The money from stove wood spanned the distance between cream and egg money and what we needed . . . like school books, shoes, overalls and shirt material, etc.

My hometown was like most small hometowns in that day . . . nestled in the upper end of a small fertile valley almost surrounded with high ridge-like mountains studded with big virgin timber that had never felt saw or axe. To the west, Gobbler Mountain with his bold ledge-like face stood like a sentinel bringing early evening shadows to the valley. Robber's Cave, a large limestone cave with legendary stories of moonshine and desperate men, was the origin of Robber's Creek . . . tumbling, jumping, and eddying its way for several miles down the canyon to the diversion gate where most of the creek was diverted to Mr. Petty's mill stream and idly flowed along the edge of the mountain to pour its tons of water over a huge over-shot water wheel that turned the stone burrs to make flour and meal or whizzed the big saw that sliced logs into lumber . . . finally returning to the creek bed, none the worse off for its service to man.

Our two churches were traditional in style; both had steeples; one—built with lumber and painted white—had stained glass. Their pastors preached with evangelistic fervor . . . pointing out the difference between right and wrong and the inescapable punishment for the wrongdoers. Church was well attended . . . some said it was partially because there was nowhere else to go.

The only school had two large rooms, an acre of playground, a well with a long pump handle, a woodshed, two outdoor accommodations marked BOYS and GIRLS. Most folks in the valley considered eight grades was enough education. If you couldn't read, write, spell, and quote all twelve multiplication tables by then you probably never could, but a handful of kids made it to the county seat and high school. A few of the well-to-do folks sent their boys to college to become lawyers or

The harvest in wagon days

doctors.

About a dozen stores made up the business and financial district which was connected with gravel sidewalks and separated about equally with a wide dirt street with a long hitch rack right down the middle.

Dr. Gullege hovered over the folks, birthing babies, setting the broken bones, patching cuts and bruises, tending the ill and the bedfast . . . relying heavily on flax seed poltices, epsom salts, turpentine and liniment.

Mr. McCullough and Mr. Marshall were friendly in public, but their general stores were fierce and bitter competitors. Between them they controlled the vote and most of the business in the valley. The only real difference in their stores was that Mr. McCullough had the post office in the left front corner of his store and furniture upstairs and handled the "Webber" wagon. Mr. Marshall was the only undertaker and had that business and his furniture in an adjoining building. He sold the "Studabaker" wagon. Otherwise, inside both stores were sorta drab . . . shelves made of 1 x 12 boards all the way to the ceiling, loaded on one side with bolts of cloth for every purpose, hat boxes, blue denim overalls and jumpers, shoe boxes, and long-legged underwear . . . to name only a few items.

At Mr. McCullough's, Mrs. Job, a sophisticated lady, wore her glasses on a string around her neck and a pencil stuck in the bun of her hair. At Marshall's, Mrs. Hickenbottom was short, stout and motherly . . . seemed to me she had more patience with boys. Both measured their cloth from thumb to nose about as fast as you could count, both dealt with the same dry goods drummers. Each tried to outdo the other by buying the very best of everything at a price country folks could afford to pay. The rest of both stores was stocked with everything from snuff to lamp chimneys, to plows, to horse collars. Both stores had a big pot-bellied stove sitting in the building the year around; a red coffee mill and a McCasky register were close to the cash drawer.

In the back there were red coal oil barrels, a babcock cream testing outfit, and a place to candle eggs . . . a back room filled with chicken coops, block salt, cream cans and empty egg cases. The familiar aroma of the mixture of new cloth, roasted coffee, cocoa, black pepper, coal oil, and chewing tobacco permeated the entire store. It was sorta enchanting . . . gave me a sense of plenty.

Outside, on Saturday, the street was muddy or dusty, hitch racks were lined with horses, wild and tame, good and bad, hitched to buggies, hacks, small spring wagons, surreys, buckboards, and heavy wagons, new and old. We never knew when a sudden gust of wind would blow a sheet of paper under the feet of a skittish horse or a dog fight might start under a team of horses. Or sometimes a sharp clap of thunder would trigger a panic that would last for hours, would destroy the serenity and tranquility of the valley for days, scattering groceries, egg cases, cream cans, and chicken coops all over town . . . and keep the horse doctor and the blacksmith busy repairing for weeks.

Model-T Fords were sorta like coyotes . . . you heard of them occasionally but you rarely saw one. When one appeared, the car and the owner were eyed with suspicion but mostly jealousy. Everybody knew they were a passing fad . . . wouldn't last long.

It all began in this valley a long time ago as a rest station for wagon trains moving west across the mountains. The trail came through Jackson's Gap and snaked its way down the side of the mountain and followed Robber's Creek to finally disappear around the bend in the distance. The lush cove-like meadows of the valley had been a haven for man and beast . . . an opportunity to repair damaged wagons, worn hubs and axles . . . to reset horse shoes and patch harness while horses grazed and rested.

America is rich in legends of the westward movement . . . accounts of raw courage are numerous. The oxen, horses, wagons, boats, barges, and rafts—fueled by an undaunted and adventurous spirit of our early eastern pioneers, but often dominated by unfriendly rivers—beat back the wilderness and conquered the streams to establish trading posts and settlements along their banks that eventually grew into huge metropolitan centers or shrank into historic landmarks.

Beyond the Mississippi it was a different story. Many of the wagon trains began at St. Louis or Kansas City. Now the westward movement was moving upstream for how far no one knew. Wild, raging, flooding streams in spring would diminish to all but non-existent in summer.

Therefore, the burden of the western movement shifted more to the wagon, water barrels, harnesses and horses. Quicksand, prairie dog holes, wind, grass, soil, mountain blizzards, scorching deserts, and a sure water hole determined the exact direction the wagon trains would take.

There were 250,000 or more hardy people from every walk of life and with every motivation . . . but all with an unwavering faith, shakeless courage and an unlimited imagination that could span the bridgeless streams, and trackless land and see the end of the rainbow out there beyond . . . under the dark clouds of the unknown.

The Santa Fe, the Butterfield, the Oregon, and the Lewis and Clark Wagon Trains and many others were beset with exhaustion, illness and accident, heartache, disappointment and failure, leaving behind relics of the covered wagon and other meager possessions.

Today what is left of their relics, their wagons, their wheels, their hubs, their pictures, their designs and their tools is held in high esteem . . . with great efforts to establish date and place of origin.

The truth, of course, is that most of those pioneers got to where they were going. The victory was sweet, and they recognized that getting there was almost reward enough. Many of them put down their roots instantly, and their accomplishments are now our heritage.

God forbid that we forget how it all happened.

PEACHES AND CREAM

The Formula: long cold winter, healthy peach trees, red sandy loam soil, weeks of bright summer sun, sprinkled often and generously with warm, gentle showers. Here is where old-fashioned peach preserves begin. Then add some old-fashioned home preserving experience.

Did you ever have a big blushing dead ripe peach drop from the limb into your hand just as you reached to pick it . . . so ripe it was real soft . . . so ripe the fuzzy skin would strip off just like the skin of a scalded tomato? Did you ever bite into a peach like that and have the juice run down and drip off your chin or run down your arms and drip off your elbows? Folks, if that didn't happen to you when you were a kid, let me tell you right now, you have missed one of the most enjoyable experiences in life and some of the finest eating Mother Nature has ever allowed the inmates of this old earth to have.

Our family orchard had apple trees, a few plum trees, and about 60 peach trees of several varieties, including

Rich sandy loam, gentle summer rains, hot summer sun and good pollenization make big blushing peaches.

Early Junes (they may have had another name, but they were the first to get ripe), Indian Clings, Elberta, Belle of Georgia, and the improved Early Hale. The Early June peaches were usually used for the table, sliced and served with sugar and cream (or sometimes ice cream). The Indian Clings were small and dusty red when ripe, beet red after they were peeled. These were always used for pickles; I'll never forget how good they were. The other varieties were used for drying, canning, and preserves.

Many of you will remember standing on a step ladder pickin' peaches while the perspiration dripped off your eyebrows, ran down your cheeks and neck. 'Member how the peach fuzz got mixed with perspiration under your clothing and itched until you could hardly bear it? Remember how the June peaches got ripe about the same time the June bugs arrived? (And remember how the June bug clawed your hand while you tied a string to his hind leg?)

The canning season was always haunted by the absence of money and the demand for Mason fruit jars and the sugar needed for canning and preserving. At our house we usually met this financial crisis by selling a few bushels of peaches to our neighbors and to Ed McCullough's store. If the fruit crop was short and we didn't have the fruit to spare, we would sell some of Mom's big Rhode Island Red hens—one was about equal to about ten pounds of sugar. On other occasions we simply split the peaches, removed the seeds, and spread them on the smokehouse roof to dry—to sweeten 'em later.

One of the symbols of this era was the cream can. I'll bet many of you will remember how the thick folds of cream were skimmed from the old stoneware crocks and poured into the cream can (the skim milk was fed to the pigs) and finally delivered to the creamery. Eager eyes watched as a sample of cream was poured into a long-necked bottle and mixed with sulphuric acid, placed into a Babcock tester and whirled at a high speed to separate the butterfat from the whey to determine the percentage of butterfat per pound of cream—on the basis of which you were paid. The results were always a topic for family discussion!

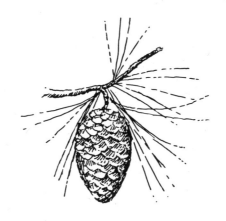

NOVEMBER 27, 1924

When I think of homemade candy, it's just like a round trip back home . . .

At milking time that particular morning a cold mist was falling from low, gloomy clouds and freezing on the board fences near the barn. The outside stock had their rumps turned to a stinging northwest wind, their shaggy coats covered with ice. It was plain to see that this Saturday would be a dreary one, and I hated the thought of going to the timber to cut wood.

My despair deepened when dad pointed out, while cleaning his boots on the back porch, that the bottoms had fallen out of the roads and the mud was nearly hub deep. That meant we wouldn't go to town that day . . . we would spend the whole day in the timber.

The prospects of two big Rhode Island hen eggs, a generous slice of ham, hot biscuits and honey for breakfast gave me new courage and boosted my morale, but it was Mom's announcement that we would make candy that night that made the day endurable. Since we would have to have fire in the cookstove to keep everything in the kitchen from freezing anyway, Mom thought we just as well make candy.

Pulling a heavy cross-cut saw, keeping a big brush pile burning, and the constant thought of making candy that night made it easy to stay warm all day. As I look back now, I think Dad had a guilt complex because he never wanted to leave a job as long as there was enough light to see. Dad knew though that the chickens would go to roost early that day and the stock needed extra care. So the day of wood cuttin' came to an end at 4:15.

My job that night as all other nights (and mornings) was to shell yellow corn from red cobs to feed the chickens. They would be nearly beside themselves when they heard the shelled corn rattle on the bottom of an old rusty bucket. Through the cracks, I could see them milling around and around the crib. The big yellow ears of corn were cold, so my hands and fingers were numb with cold by the time I had finished. Of course, I was rewarded a little later when I gathered five or six dozen big brown eggs from the henhouse and barn. Besides, I had a bucket of red cobs for kindling too.

(At chore time during those boyhood years, I revealed a lot of ambitious plans and described many of my boyish air castles to those chickens and livestock. The chickens would cock their heads sideways and blink their eyes; the old cows would examine me with a sort of bewildered look, but they never betrayed my secrets or divulged my plans. As a result, most of those plans and ideas are resting in the archives of memories 'til this day.)

The stock were cold and hungry; the cows were bawling for their calves and anxious to get in shelter. It was just a matter of opening the barn doors. While I milked in the flickering yellow light of an old coal-oil lantern, Dad fed the hogs and forked some bright yellow oats from the loft to feed the stock when the cows had finished their bran. The cows' fleecy-haired udders were tight with milk and they were glad to give it down.

The sights, sounds, and smells of a stock barn at the close of a cold, damp, and dreary day may be best understood by a ten or twelve-year-old farm boy: the strong odor of shivering and steaming bodies, the stifling dust of clean straw bedding, and the sweet smell of blackstrap molasses in mixed feed rations, the cozy sounds of pigeons talking to one another, the chirping sparrows getting settled for the night, horses crunching hard corn, cows licking their calves' rumps or feed boxes, the smacking sounds of sucking calves, the first few streams of milk spraying on the bottoms of an empty milk bucket soon to be muffled by foam rising from rich warm milk, the spooky shadows of dusty cobwebs clinging to the rough loft joists, a brindle cat walking proudly along a narrow sill with a squeaking mouse in her mouth, the thumping of a sucking calf's tail against its mother's ribs . . . all strange to most of the world but contentment to a small farm boy.

Then there was the woodbox, and it was always empty. It seemed that the "badder" the weather or the "tireder" I was, the more wood those old stoves would burn, and that night the weather was bad and I was tired. Only the anticipation of the candy making made it possible for me to load my red wagon with split cook wood and pull it through the freezing mist to the house. Mom complained about the wood being wet, said it would put the fire out. She threatened to skin me if I got loose bark all over the floor. I didn't know how to avoid either problem. This was drudgery in the worst form that I knew anything about, but it wouldn't be long now 'til candy making and pan lickin' . . . an hour or so.

Mom and I didn't agree on my face washing that night either. After three washings she suggested it would have been better to wash the dirt off rather than wipe it off on

119

her good towel.

Sometime during the day Mom must have trimmed the wicks and polished the chimneys of both our coal-oil lamps. Their yellow flame was even and steady that night. After my blundering around the woodpile in the dim light of a coal-oil lantern, the lamps seemed bright and cheery. With both the cookstove and the heating stove going, the old house was pretty warm except around the drafty door.

The aroma of ham-hock and navy beans and crackling cornbread appealed to my empty stomach. I went a little easy on supper though because I didn't want to fill up on everyday food when there was going to be homemade candy and pans to lick.

After supper Dad picked up the bi-weekly *St. Louis Globe Democrat* which had found its way across the Ozark mountains to our house in only three days. With his long legs astraddle the heating stove, the brightest of our two lamps on a table back of his chair, he was soon absorbed in the current events. He considered the *Globe* the law and gospel and shaped his arguments to defend its integrity and accuracy.

A trip to the back porch with a washpan for walnuts and hickory nuts started the festivities. While a gusty northwest wind whistled through the cracks in the attic and rubbed the stiff oak limbs against the gable of our old house, I cracked the nuts on a flat iron with a bright horse-shoe nail. When a mislick shattered hickory nut hulls on the floor, Dad lowered his paper long enough to tell me, in no uncertain terms, the outcome if those shells were left on the floor for him to walk barefooted on the next morning when he built a fire.

When Mom began toasting nuts and melting chocolate, I had trouble staying out of her way. I could hardly wait for the first spoon and kettle to lick . . . if there is anything more fun and better eatin' than that I haven't run onto it yet.

I didn't understand it then, but I have discovered since that it takes real butter, real cream, real eggs and lots of nutmeats to make candy taste like that candy tasted and make a kitchen smell like that kitchen smelled that night.

Mom made four or five kinds of candy—more than we could eat in several days. I knew without asking that she would share it with the neighbors tomorrow.

... Only two hours of candy making but twelve hours of a gloomy day made bright with anticipation by a wise, thoughtful mother on November 27, 1924 ... Mom's birthday that Dad and I had forgotten.

CHURNIN'

The milkin' lot, about twenty yards wide and thirty-five yards long, had been built many years ago. The split oak posts, leaning critically, had withstood the onslaughts of fighting cows and playing calves. The unpainted, 1 x 6 inch planks had been split, broken, patched, and renailed many times and were now sagging under the sheer weight of abuse and years. The board gate, swinging from a large hand-hewn post, cutting a narrow furrow into a perfect circle as the gate was opened and closed daily.

Hanging on pegs in the corner of the lot were three milk stools: two with one leg and one with three legs—with a certain antique finish, the results of being exposed to the seat of blue denim overalls and a calico dress fourteen times a week. In another corner of the lot, a short post had been driven into the ground and an improvised box nailed to its battered top . . . this was the salt box. I can't think of a more melodious sound than the rhythmic toll of a cow bell while the bell cow licked a block of salt.

The lane that led from the lot to the open pasture was flanked on the right by a five-strand barbed wire fence separating the cows from a fine old orchard including several Jonathan, Sweet Apple, Winesap, York Imperials, Arkansas Blacks, Ben Davis, Grimes Golden, and several others. (These trees provided the apples for my favorite teachers at Bellview School for many years.) A four-foot woven wire fence on the left side of the lane, defended the big garden from the cows and chickens, but showed the strain of the cows trying to reach the tender shoots of the gooseberry and raspberry bushes through the fence. Heavy traffic between the milk lot and the pasture restricted the vegetation to wire grass, dog fennel, ragweed, and bull thistle.

The pasture was several acres situated on sort of a plateau, sliced several times by the upper ends of deep-cut ravines that led to the river, covered by heavy timber once, but now only a few second growth trees . . . a lush pasture of orchard grass, Jap clover, and many wild grasses.

Many of you will remember that it was a real chore to wade through the tall, dew-laden grass and follow your ear to a distant cow bell on a crisp fall morning . . . barefooted. Your toes would be numb with cold by the time you found the cows. Remember how you warmed your feet by standing a while where an old cow had slept all night . . . a real source of comfort, wasn't it?

At our place there was "Old Maude," the bell cow, a Holstein. She was big and always hungry, had unsightly horns, a bossy disposition . . . which made her kinda hard to milk, but she was good for a 2½ gallon bucket of milk night and morning. "Old Bess" was a medium-sized roan with a nice disposition; she kicked occasionally when her teats were briar-scratched—and was good for about four gallons a day, but would milk over a longer period than Maude. "Daisy" was short and fairly wide—a cross between Guernsey and something else; she gave about four gallons of rich, golden-colored milk a day. She had a fine disposition and always had fine calves. "Tiny" was a small, timid Jersey with sharp horns, a meek disposition, long teats, easy to milk; she gave about 3½ to 4 gallons a day which tested 5½ to 6 per cent butterfat, and she nearly always had fine heifer calves. As a family, we probably loved her best. We kids called her "Ready" because we could milk her any time between two and six every Sunday evening to make ice cream after we returned from the swimming hole. Of course, we had other cows, yearlings and spring calves too, but I remember these cows best.

The day began and ended about the same every day on the farm. We hit the floor at 5:30 a.m.—feeding chickens, milking, currying, and harnessing the horses, then to breakfast of country-cured ham, eggs swimming in ham fryings, with biscuits, real cow butter, country sorghum, and cold milk or coffee. Then followed a half day of real toil, with dinner at 12:00—another real meal—then another half day of genuine labor, then more chores and another real meal. Calories—? diets—? we never heard of such things; hard work and long hours took care of everything—kept you lean and rugged.

The weeks began and ended about the same, too. Monday was washday, the day that we ate leftovers from Sunday. There were no washing machines then much. Our equipment included a copper-bottom wash boiler, two galvanized tubs, a washboard, homemade soap, and "boughtin" blueing.

Tuesday and Wednesday were the days when Mom ironed, worked in the garden, canned fruits and vegetables, made jelly, preserves ... in summer. Fall and winter, Tuesdays and Wednesdays were the days she patched, ironed, quilted, tacked comforts, made head cheese and sausage, mincemeat and butters from dried apples and peaches.

Thursday was butter day. At our house, milk was strained into big stoneware milk crocks (one, one and a half, and two gallon sizes). In warm weather, these crocks of milk were kept in a long, split-log trough in the wellhouse. Every time someone went by the wellhouse, they would draw a bucket of cold water and pour in the trough. This would hold the temperature down. (There were no refrigerators in those days . . . not at our house, anyway.) Every morning the cream was skimmed from the crocks. I can see it yet: as Mom would draw the spoon around the edge of the crock, the big heavy layer of cream would wrinkle into big thick folds and be ladled off into our churn. (The skimmed milk would be fed to the pigs.) The churn was kept in the milk trough, too, until there was enough for a "churnin'."

Churnin' was my job, you see, and always required more patience than I had. Sometimes I'd sit on the kitchen stool awhile, then stand on one leg, then the other. Kr-chug-kr-chug went the old dasher. Mom would check it now and then . . . add a cup of warm or cold water, whichever one she thought it needed, and say, "It's made, just needs gatherin' "—whatever that meant. It was at this point that I learned a great lesson. Sometimes I enjoyed this chore; most of the time, I didn't. I discovered the job didn't change much, but my attitude did . . . I have found this to be true in about every other job I have tried in life.

Mom was a good hand at working butter; she used an old wooden butter paddle to work the milk out and the salt in. Then she worked the butter into round wooden butter molds and dropped it on wax paper. I'll never forget . . . her mold had a big butternut carved into the top. The top of every pound of butter would have the image of a butternut. The finished butter was carefully placed into a large wooden bucket and tied to a long rope. We would let it down into our dug well where it

The good life includes bare feet, good fruit and a puckered smile.

was about 45 to 50 degrees; this was our refrigerator in the summer.

Friday was baking day, the day I enjoyed most. I can still smell that bread when it was taken from the oven of the old wood range, the crust moistened with that golden homemade butter. Boy! what an aroma!

Saturday morning was the time we tried to finish everything that we had started during the week. Then we went to town Saturday "evening." Ed McCullough had the big store and some of the best trade in town. He would take all the butter we could make, all our eggs, all the frying chickens we could spare, plus squash, cucumbers, green beans, etc.

Among my most vivid recollections are the fall times of childhood. About apple pickin' time, it seemed more exciting than usual. By this time, most of the fruit jars were filled with vine-ripened fruits and vegetables. The warm autumn sun and the cool nights of September had arrived. The apples were taking on gorgeous bright colors. Under the trees, the windfalls had begun to spoil. The yellow jackets and bees were busy getting their share of the crop. Stepladders were standing close around the trees. Dad and others were busy gathering the fragrant apples in a canvas sack strapped around their necks and backs. The choice apples would be put in baskets and stored; odd shapes and sizes would be made into cider; others would be dried. Mom would core and slice the apples. The thin slices would be spread on muslin cloth on the smokehouse roof and covered with some kind of material that looked like curtains to keep off the yellow jackets and bees.

Apple and peach butter time: that was the time when it was cold outside, and we needed the stove going anyway. Mom figured about 75 per cent apples and 25 per cent sugar—with a dash of cinnamon and allspice. There were two reasons she made it this way—we had the apples but had to buy the sugar (that ought to have been reason enough), but she thought it was better butter that way, too. The apples and sugar mixture was put over a slow fire, let simmer—it would blubber and spatter all over everything. We kids would steer clear for fear we would get spattered on. Mom would let it cook down 'til it got thick and had a certain sheen—boy, it sure was good!

LIBERTY BELL

The desk represented more lumber than skill; the chair suggested strength rather than design. They sat on a 6 x 8 foot platform that was about 12 inches high in front of two large pictures, one of Christopher Columbus and the other of George Washington, separated by our flag. This was the first view of authority that the boy must recognize and respect.

The one-room school sat in a cove overlooking a broad, serene, and fertile valley that was farmed by the sons of the original settlers. The boy's one-room cabin home overlooked the valley from a high limestone ledge that was at the end and the top of a long, crooked trail that led up the steep mountainside.

That day I knew him so well, that boy. He was six; his overalls were patched and faded. His blue shirt was homemade and the tail was dangling from the unbuttoned sides of his overalls. His bare feet were covered with skinned places and mud stains. His blue eyes sparkled through a freckled smile from under the ragged brim of an old straw hat. I thought for a moment he recognized me, but "old" Carlo, his beagle, licked his hand for attention. The boy rumpled the beagle's ears and went off to romp and wrestle. I wanted to shout to him, but, as if in a dream, I couldn't; I wanted to visit with him awhile because it would be many miles, many mountains and valleys, oceans and continents, many heartaches and joys and many tears and laughter before he caught up with me. For the man and the boy he was don't come together again except when the rare time of reverie comes during the Indian summer of his own life.

The boy's world for most of his first six years was within the split-rail fence that skirted the limestone ledge and surrounded his cabin. He was the product of dedicated rural-born parents who were poor, but respected, reliable, and enduring, with a deep faith and trust in God. To them the words *convenience* and *greed* were unknown.

Their needs were so great . . . their income so meager, but rarely was jealousy and selfishness observed. They were driven by an unwavering faith in America . . . well versed in her history from 1492 to Jamestown and Plymouth to the embattled farmers at Concord Bridge. Making choices was simple: what they wanted was either homegrown, homemade, or they did without. But whatever the price, they were willing to pay because everything would be all right someday . . . always out there someday.

So, in due time the boy, too, would share their faith and spirit. He would learn that it was the same four calloused hands that spanked and caressed him . . . the same four untiring arms that would hug and switch him . . . the same two voices that expressed love and authority. It would be these parents who would plant the seeds of moral courage that would help shape his destiny and strengthen the faith and spirit that were so necessary to make a life worthwhile.

The morning of the first Monday in September 1919: the boy was scrubbed and polished . . . dressed in new overalls and shirt, with a book, tablet, pencils, crayons, book satchel, and a half-gallon syrup bucket for a lunch pail . . . ready for the first day of school.

It seems right now I am leaning against that rail fence watching the boy . . . somehow I can't cross the rail fence to join him, though I wish I could. I would like to take his hand in mine and walk down the rocky mountain trail together. We could smell the fragrance of the damp autumn breeze; we could hear the rustling of the tired oak leaves and the impatient sound of Robber's Creek rushing onward to somewhere. I would like to sit on the flat rock near the schoolhouse door and watch him pry the lid off the syrup bucket dinner pail and see him bite into the sweaty sandwiches.

The trail would lead him to the valley below where a faithful teacher in a one-room schoolhouse would transplant reading, writing, and arithmetic from the books to his mind and enrich the soil where the seeds of moral courage were already planted by his parents.

I like to think about the boy and his life . . . the eagerness of his inquiry, to explore, to investigate, to pretend. I like to remember the day he delivered his first quart of milk from his own cow for a nickel and the free enterprise spirit was born. The muscles of ambition and vision were flexed with immediate plans for expansion. The sale of five *Saturday Evening Post* subscriptions for a set of binoculars. The time his Dad helped him build a "box" rabbit trap and the sale of dressed cotton-tail rabbits delivered for 25¢ each. The first job at age 12 away from home at the general store testing the butterfat content of cream . . . candling eggs . . . weighing chickens. The sale of a white-face calf for $12.50 and the purchase of a secondhand bicycle with the money. The magnitude of this transaction opened new vistas and triggered dreams of leaving the cabin on the limestone ledge when he grew up . . . to go beyond Gobbler Mountain to the great places that books had spoken of . . . to build a great empire somewhere on the distant horizon of time and space.

One day he did leave the cabin and the serene valley. He took the trail across Robber's Creek and over Gobbler Mountain through Jackson Gap. The trail grew wider and a little smoother . . . and the magnitude, magnificence, and the splendor of America began to unfold.

For the next forty years he traveled every major highway and every airlane to almost every city and town, standing in awe as he visited the landmarks, shrines, and monuments that honored a great people whose lives, deprivations, courage, and wisdom had shaped the destiny of America.

He learned of the history of this land . . . how four attempts to establish colonies in America failed before 1607. One was Roanoke Island, North Carolina in 1585 where Virginia Dare was born in August 1587, the first child of English parents to be born in America. This colony disappeared without a trace and has been since known as the Lost Colony.

At Jamestown it was the story of a colony of poorly prepared Englishmen in three frail ships sailing north four days out of the Caribbean, being bashed ashore by a sudden and contrary gale, to what eventually became James River and Jamestown. On the morning of May 14, 1607, when the storm subsided, they went ashore and began building a fort that was named for King James, the first permanent English settlement in America. By the following spring only 38 of the original colonists were alive. Midway the previous winter 120 more colonists, just as unprepared, had arrived. In April another colony arrived. In 18 months half of all the colonies had died. An innocent and inexperienced people were building Jamestown in a swamp. The heat, bad water and poor food were the main culprits. However, there were the gentlemen who refused to work, artisans who were afraid to get dirty, others just lazy and indolent, thus John Smith's decree "anyone who doesn't work, doesn't eat." Each man must work as hard as the president and produce as much food or be banished from the fort until he amended his behavior or starved. John Smith's stern command saved the colony, but in August, nine crippled sailing ships with almost 500 new and unprepared settlers arrived. Through ignorance they stirred up the Indians and questioned Smith's authority. Wounded in a gunpowder accident, he sailed for England. And sensing the weakness of the leadership, the Indians became dangerously bold. The corn supply was cut off; the barter system was abolished.

John Smith had left 500 colonists at Jamestown. Six months later only sixty were alive; by June it was discovered that provisions for 16 days remained . . . not enough for a voyage to England, but they would sail north hoping to be picked up by fishing boats off the coast of Newfoundland. On June 10, 1610 Jamestown was abandoned, but at that moment Thomas West and three-hundred new colonists and a year of supplies sailed into the Bay . . . that saved the day and Jamestown.

Though the price was high, the success of those first English Americans largely determined the future ownership, population, language, and culture of a great portion of the North American continent that would become the United States in about 168 years.

The boy at Plymouth Rock found much the same story as he grasped the guard rails and viewed the traditional rock, trying fully to imagine, though totally unable to do so, life on the tiny Mayflower, crossing the harsh and ruthless Atlantic, the long sailing, the sickness, the almost unbearable conditions . . . sustained only by raw courage and the undaunted faith and hope of a new day in a new world. The Pilgrims were as unprepared for what they found as the colonists of Jamestown. Instead of an easy living and quick wealth, they found a savage climate . . . a beautiful but unfriendly and untamed land that would cost them the most of their lives. In the following 168 years, the good news of the new world spread and people came and had children, and the population grew to 2½ million people. By 1771 America was buying over $4,000,000 in goods from England annually and selling in return about $1½ million. This trade deficit was deeply resented as were certain taxation and other restrictions and boundaries. Eventually nearly every transaction in America moved on credit controlled by England. In April 1775 the Continental Congress opened the American ports to most of the world.

American colonists were not an oppressed people, as often believed. Their economic opportunities and personal liberties were among the best in the world at that time. They were, however, keenly aware of the sacrifice and deprivation . . . the price that had been paid by their forefathers over the 168 years in the new world. As their dreams blossomed into hard-earned reality they became possessive, suspicious, self-reliant and fiercely independent . . . any threat to their dreams or affairs was taken as seriously as if they had a bayonet against their throats.

The real causes for the Revolution were hard to explain, but "fighting for liberty" was emotional, patriotic, and acceptable. A year before the Declaration of Independence, the Continental Congress issued a declaration explaining why they were doing such an outrageous thing as rebelling against England. "We have counted the cost of this contest and find nothing so dreadful as voluntary slavery" wrote Thomas Jefferson. "Honor, justice and humanity forbid us tamely to surrender that Freedom which we received from our gallant ancestors, and which our innocent posterity have a right to receive from us," Congress said in a Declaration of Causes and Necessities for Taking Up Arms that was adopted on July 6, 1775.

Although independence had been months, even years, coming to an audible expression, the heart and spirit of the country had longed for it from the beginning.

March 23, 1776 Patrick Henry, a great orator, born in the backwoods of Virginia, raised on the edge of civilization, mostly self-taught, denounced British rule with his famous speech, "Is life so dear, or peace so sweet, as to be purchased at the price of chains and slavery? Forbid it, Almighty God, I know not what course others will take, but as for me, give me Liberty or give me Death." About three weeks later 700 British regulars clashed with the minutemen at Lexington Green, then were turned back at Concord Bridge, with casualities of over 90 Americans and 270 British. June 15, 1779 Congress appointed George Washington Commander-in-Chief of the Continental Army. August 23rd King George accused America of "open and avowed rebellion." June 7, 1776, 14½ months after the clash at Lexington, Richard Henry Lee of Virginia offered a resolution that the colonies, "Are and of right ought to be, free and independent states." The resolution was generally opposed, but Congress resolved to try again. June 11, Thomas Jefferson, 33 years old, a second-year delegate, was elected to a committee of five that included John Adams, 40, Benjamin Franklin, 70, Roger Sherman, 35, and Robert Livingston, 29, to draft a Declaration of Independence.

Between June 11 and 28, 1776, in a sweltering rented room on the second floor of a bricklayer's home at the corner of Market and Seventh streets in Philadelphia, Thomas Jefferson penned the first draft of what would become a monument in the literature of human liberty. Jefferson presented the draft to Franklin and Adams who suggested three or four minor changes. Jefferson then presented it to the committee of five ... without change, it was presented to the Congress June 28.

At dawn on Tuesday, July 2, 1776, it was overcast and threatening. Jefferson noted the 70 degree temperature with high humidity. A short time after daylight a sharp clap of thunder introduced a cloudburst that drenched the city of 40,000. By nine o'clock nearly 50 delegates to the second Continental Congress had filled the ground floor of the State House. Conversations were low and subdued; quick glances identified every person entering the building. With the windows closed against the rain, the odor from a nearby stable made the room stifling. One could sense the anticipation and the tensions. It seemed that something eternal was in the balance.

When Richard Henry Lee's resolution was first read on June 7, it was generally opposed. The day before (July 1), a preliminary vote on Lee's resolution showed nine colonies in favor, two (South Carolina and Pennsylvania) opposed, with New York abstaining and Delaware deadlocked. To decide such momentous business—cutting much of a continent and its 2½ million people free from the British Empire—the delegates hoped for a unanimous vote. Anything less might be fertile soil for disunity.

A whispered rumor traveled through the hall that Pennsylvania had changed positions and would vote for the resolution. South Carolina's Edward Rutledge entered the hall smiling. His colony, too, would vote for independence. New York, still waiting for instructions, would not dissent. Only Delaware was left—stalemated—one delegate in favor, the other opposed. John Hancock, president of the Congress, rapped his gavel; secretary Charles Thomson began rereading the resolution aloud prior to a vote. Then over the cobblestone street outside came the clatter of horse's hoofs; water-soaked and muddy, his face twisted with pain and fatigue, Delaware's third delegate, Caesar Rodney, had ridden all night to cover the 80 miles between Dover and Philadelphia after an express rider told him of his colony's stalemate. He wore a handkerchief over the lower part of his face to cover a consuming cancer. "The thunder and rain delayed me," Rodney casually explained as he entered the room. There without dissent the colonies of America took the long step that severed the 169-year-old political ties with the mother country proclaiming that they "are, and of right ought to be, free and independent states" . . . INDEPENDENCE, a process as painful and bloody as birth.

The Statue of Liberty and Ellis Island have been mute witnesses to tens of millions of freedom-hungry people seeking for whatever "Life, Liberty, and the Pursuit of Happiness" means to them. As the boy viewed the vast Atlantic through the crown of the Statue of Liberty, his imagination pierced the misty horizon to hear the story about America, spoken in many languages and dialects from all over the world. But the story always ended the same: "If we could only find a way." Only a relatively few brought wealth with them. Most brought meager possessions, national or regional characteristics, family traits, prejudices, and religious, political, and cultural convictions and, of course, memories of family ties . . . the tears and waving hands as the ships lifted anchor.

The boy, turning half around, saw the same, strange, gaunt faces funneling through Ellis Island Immigration Center . . . faces that expressed fear of the unknown, the desperation of survival, of being on their own from that moment on. But back of it all were faith and hope that would make the misery of life a little easier until a better life would come to them in the new world some day. As the boy took the last look from the Statue of Liberty, the flags surrounding the Bay were unfurling in a gentle breeze, and he envisioned they were still beckoning people to a great country. As he descended the long stairs to the elevators below he realized that since 1492, nearly 500 years, people had been coming to these shores. The pain and sacrifice had been excruciating to some, but on the whole the country and the free enterprise system had been good to millions.

The Industrial Revolution began in England in the 1760's . . . about 50 years later, it began to catch on in the new world. Sensing the approach of that era, Thomas Jefferson noted that "agriculture, manufacture, commerce, and navigation, the four pillars of our prosperity are the most thriving when left to individual enterprise." Every school child knows that the revolution was a struggle for freedom. What is often overlooked is that one of the basic liberties for which the colonies fought was the freedom of enterprise. The freedom to do business . . . to develop and manufacture and market without economic constraints imposed by England. The United States was now destined to be the largest and best source for every human need in the world. To do that would require people . . . millions of them, their trades, their experience, their wisdom and muscle.

As the ferry returned to Manhattan, everywhere the boy looked there was a mountain of concrete and steel shaped to please the taste of man, housing business and commerce. He entertained the thought of how it had looked when it was a wilderness. Heading west, going under the Hudson River through the Holland tunnels, the concrete ribbons wound their way across the land of history, mountains of coal mines, through a beautiful countryside spotted with factory and farm. Each bridge he crossed was a reminder that one day a frontier scout had searched miles for a river crossing safe for the western movement of people.

The boy, coming home in the Indian summer of his life, remembered the day he left his cabin home on the limestone ledge, took the trail across Robber's Creek and over Gobbler Mountain through Jackson Gap to seek his fortune. The magnitude, magnificence, and the splendor of America had indeed unfolded.

America's face is blemished, her heart is scarred, but her pulse and will are strong; faith and courage are bold; her vision is good, and America is as promising as in the beginning.

After 40 years, the cabin home was only a memory, the one-room school was a memory, too. The leaning livestock sheds and haystacks had been replaced with huge white and red barns; red brick colonial homes had replaced small white cottages. The clotheslines and piles of firewood were gone; white propane tanks sat in their place. White mailboxes were in front of most homes instead of in a cluster at a distant corner of the road. Dusty roads and lanes were now black-topped ... the ridges were shrouded with an autumn touch. Tired oak leaves were fluttering to the ground. The lowing of mother cows searching for their calves could be heard in the distance. The serenity and tranquility of the valley remaining the same, only the bold ledge-like face of Gobbler Mountain was changeless.

For as long as it is Indian summer in my life, somewhere inside me will be the boy who wonders and dreams, sees visions and whistles and meanders down along an eternal trail.

A country telephone in operation

JIM AND LUCY'S PHONE

Alexander Graham Bell, 1847-1922, invented the telephone in 1876. There is no estimate of how many telephones have been manufactured in the 100 years that have followed. But it is said that there are more than 358 million in use throughout the world—about one-half of them in the United States—and well over 325 million miles of telephone wire stretched over the earth to carry the message.

49F13 was our number ... one long and three short rings. The phone was made of oak and stained a little; the mouthpiece, receiver, bells, and crank were black. It hung on the wall between the sheet-iron heating stove and the stand table where Mom kept a sparkling clean kerosene lamp. The phone was in the most conspicuous place in the house . . . and was our proudest possession indeed.

Over 50 years have gone by since we installed the phone; I don't remember the transaction and the politics involved, but I remember Dad had to clear the right-of-way and cut and set the poles. Then the day came when two men unrolled the wire; another man with metal spikes strapped to his legs would run up and down those poles like a cat. (I imagined how those spikes would be a big help when squirrel hunting.) Finally the wire was stretched, the phone was fastened to the wall, and the ground wire driven into the damp earth. Then one of the men cranked the phone four or five times and when a voice came on the line, he asked if she could hear him. Then he asked her to ring our number . . . almost instantly we heard one long and three shorts, our very own number, ringing on our own personal phone. How she could ring those little bells all the way from town was far more than we could understand.

We now had the privilege of calling anyone who had a phone or could be called to a phone for $1.50 a month . . . our first monthly obligation to meet. That night Mom examined the "directory," a folder that had a handful of phone numbers. She began to call those folks she knew; somewhere in the conversation she would mention the phone in a sort of off-handed way. Then to the all-important question, she would answer, "Oh, yes! we have a phone . . . you must call anytime you can."

I learned later there were five or six other phones on our line, and Mom would listen in every time any number rang for fear the folks weren't home or that central had erred in ringing the number. It was a lame excuse, but it seemed to sooth Mom's conscience.

The first 16 years of my life we lived on the edge

of the river breaks and the big timber country; having the only phone in a mountain country meant the people could, and would, come at all times of the day and night to use our phone to summon help, a doctor, etc. It meant our home must never be locked.

Mom and Dad always felt it their sacred trust to soften the blow of fate and give spiritual guidance to those who may have strayed. So the time of day or what we were doing or the weather had little to do with the mission when a call came. Sometimes it was I who would carry the message of heartbreak or joy, on a note written by my mother, through the mountain trails no wider than a horse, on foot by lantern light, or on horseback, to some distant neighbor. Telephone messages in those days were like letters edged in black. They usually meant bad news. Whether good or bad news, there was a hush when Mom's notes were opened, an agonizing tension, a reflection of fear and uncertainty on their lean faces, accented by the deep shadows made from a flickering kerosene lamp or fireplace. Then a sigh of relief to good news. If it were bad news, a discussion of what to do next . . . sometimes another note, a call to take back to Mom. If the news were good, everything would be all right for me going home; if it were bad, Molly's friendly neigh was more comforting. The hoot owls seemed closer, the night sounds seemed more strange and foreboding, creeks seemed deeper and the water colder, but the squeaky saddle, Molly's damp sweaty flesh and the steady pace of her well-shod feet knocking the fire out of the rocks gave me the security I needed. Regardless of the time we arrived home, Molly was paid in full with a big yellow ear of corn and a handful of oat hay; she always seemed pleased. I would fall in bed feeling I had been responsible, important, and manly.

The farmer's barter system gave way to cash and credit and he was no longer in charge of his destiny.

Mom's mission usually began when a neighbor came to use "Jim and Lucy's phone" to call Dr. Gullege. Hours later "Old Doc" would arrive at our house in his black buggy pulled by a beautiful dapple-gray mare. All three would be covered with dust or mud. Mom would join him to help in the case and keep Doc on the right buggy trails. There were lots of accidents and mishaps that could befall mountain people, so Mom carried her Bible, two bed sheets, a comb and brush because she never knew how long her services would be needed. Once when I asked what was wrong with Mrs. Kelso, she said, "None of your business." This was before boys knew where babies came from. But I learned when she said that it would be a day or two before she returned . . . Dad and I would batch.

In those days, the cure for most ills was brews, potions, and poltices handed down by ancestors, epsom salts and castor oil. Sulphur and molasses were reliable, too. The truth though was that most ills were not cured but were worn out by a strong body.

When young Doc Gullege arrived in our hometown, he was promptly challenged by the home remedies, and he never quite conquered them. Except for accidents, Doc wasn't called until all the home remedies failed. He had to be pretty smart to substitute his science for leaves, roots, and bark of herbs.

Socially Doc was at the top and bottom . . . more important than the banker in time of trouble and less important than a hired hand when it came to paying for his trip. If he had been paid all that was due him, he would have built a fortune in this lifetime because he didn't have time to spend the money. Instead he was paid in part with stove wood, hams, bacon, eggs, potatoes, turnips, corn and hay and "conscience money" occasionally.

One time I heard Doc Gullege tell Mom that he appreciated her help . . . that she had a natural knack for helping people . . . that people would learn to respect her wisdom. Mom believed what he said and devoted the remainder of her life to that point of view.

THE TEACHER'S APPLE

Things were looking up at our house. In just a few short years we had made enough money on strawberries to move from our one-room, rough clapboard cabin to a new rough board-and-batten house with two unfinished rooms upstairs and two rooms downstairs with a connecting ladder. And now we had traded our 40-acre hill farm for 35 acres of upland that was almost level . . . with an impressive house with two unfinished rooms upstairs and three rooms downstairs with a connecting stairway, a lean-to kitchen and a screened-in porch. Our new house had been painted outside and papered downstairs . . . once . . . a long time ago.

Our new farm had conveniences too: a well, a dug well, four feet in diameter and 80 feet deep, a wellhouse, a pulley, a rope with an oaken bucket on each end (and only a hundred yards from the back door—this beat the spring branch at the bottom of a steep ravine a quarter of a mile from the house that we were used to). There was also an unpainted barn with stalls for two horses, two cows, a corn crib and cobwebs. This time we had a hen house too . . . with a leaky roof . . . that would accommodate nearly 100 hens. We had a front yard and big rockless garden that had been taken over with stubborn Bermuda grass. Just north of the barn were about 50 old—but big and healthy—apple trees that represented eight or ten varieties (most that I had never heard of) including Jonathan, Arkansas Blacks, Ben Davis, York Imperials and Black Twiggs.

In the meantime I had survived my first year at Mason School; many of my lessons had been painful. I had sat on the teacher's desk facing the kids for fighting, stood at the blackboard with my nose in a chalk circle for whispering. I had been soundly whipped with a tree limb for sassing. But somehow I had lived through it all and passed . . . by a narrow margin. Now for my second year I faced a new and a bigger challenge . . . Bellview School.

To Dad, God was powerful . . . was in heaven and ran an itemized account of each individual's behavior . . . to determine reward or punishment when the time came. Mom's relationship with God was personal and intimate. She believed the Lord was by her side constantly guiding her destiny. She shared her problems with Him on her knees by her bedside. Sometimes when I saw her tear-stained eyes, I thought the Lord had shared some of the world's problems with her, too. She had a sharp definition of right and wrong, and all human behavior was one or the other. She insisted on supporting the Lord's work with her tithes. This rarely meant money . . . more often it was one yellow-legged frying rooster out of ten, one dozen big brown eggs out of ten dozen, one pound of yellow butter out of ten, etc. She considered humility a great virtue and gave God and others full credit for all the good things in life.

So moving to our new farm was approached with caution and self-examination just to be sure we were not unduly proud or exalted. After all, it was a $1,100 farm; we were the folks that had bought the Spencer place.

Mom and Dad thought it was a great relief to get away from the rocky soil of the "old homeplace." They were eager to tackle the rockless, level land. To their sorrow, however, they learned that Bermuda grass could spread in a garden faster than they could dig it up. Some of the "lush pasture" turned out to be wet, sour land that would grow nothing but wire grass that was so tough that stock couldn't bite it. The "beautiful" meadow turned out to have a good stand of sage grass that was hated by both man and beast.

Mom's and Dad's vision penetrated and went beyond their discouragements; out beyond they could see orchards, vineyards and the horn of plenty of their 35 acres. They would run the risk and wait for a better day.

Aside from fighting Bermuda grass and praying for rain we spent the summer getting acquainted with our new neighbors and friends. We learned that Bellview was a much bigger school than Mason . . . 28 or 29 kids instead of 17. We learned that Miss Patterson was going to be the new teacher that fall . . . that she and a Mr. Hobbs, a neighborhood man, were going to be married. This was thought to be an economic advantage by the school board . . . since she would not have to pay room and board. Her contract called for $35 per month instead of $45 and would last until the money ran out . . . five or six months, maybe.

148

After a year's experience with having a son in school, Dad came up with what he called a new policy. It was short and simple: if I got a licking at school, I could expect another one when I got home. He wanted it clearly understood that he would have no part in raising a "criminal." This new policy seemed to me cruel and unjust . . . but I knew he meant it.

About the same time Mom inaugurated what ought to have been called a "Teacher-Student Relationship Program." From the minute she learned that Miss Patterson was going to be the new teacher, she pointed out, what seemed to be hourly, at least daily, what a lucky kid I was to have Miss Patterson as a teacher. She was a wonderful lady coming a long way just to teach me. If I would pay attention to her, I would learn something . . . and grow up to be a businessman some day. By the time school started, she had convinced me that Miss Patterson was not only very smart . . . she was flawless.

An all night's rain, Sunday night September 16 ended the drought, cooled the air and converted the dust to mud. Monday morning was bright and rich with anticipation: it would be the first day of school at Bellview.

Drought and hard times had delayed new shoes and a new dinner pail. But I did have new overalls (folded to the knees), a white shirt, a blue denim book satchel, secondhand books, a tablet, crayons, pencils, etc.

Armed with a year's experience, Dad's new policy, Mom's fine opinion of Miss Patterson, a half gallon syrup bucket filled with peanut butter sandwiches and leftover fried chicken, I faced the new challenge with assurance and determination.

The path through the orchard was lined with wet grass that felt cool and refreshing to my bare feet. The tired leaves on the big apple trees were still dripping from last night's rain; the air was freighted with the odor

149

No trouble here

of mature grass and windfall apples. The ground was covered with apples that had been blown off of the trees by the wind during the night.

I paused long enough to choose two bright red Jonathans from the grass. I picked the tickle grass from their wet red skins and polished both on my overalls and stowed them in my hind pocket. A few yards later I found a big Black Twigg apple in the path . . . it was also red and perfect. I polished it on my overalls too, pried the lid off my syrup bucket lunch pail and stowed it away. I met Virgil, my cousin, at the corner of Job's Woods, and we approached Bellview together.

Bellview, as the name implies, was located on a prairie-like plateau in about the center of an acre of land that was used for a playground. The school was big to me . . . 35 x 40 feet maybe, with four windows on each side, a door in the middle of the front with two improvised limestone steps beneath it, a belfry and a big rusty bell. A red brick flue ran up the back on the outside and was finished sorta fancy two or three feet above the ridge row. It was plain to see the old schoolhouse had resisted the wind and the rain—and withstood the wear and tear of rough-necked kids—a long time.

It was a little different inside. A new layer of pretty paper had been hung with unprofessional skill. The window casing and the wainscoating were painted off-white; the floors were oily and clean. The big heating stove, sitting toward the back, had a new coat of stove black; the stovepipe had a few new joints and was supported with bailing wire that ran from the pipe to the ceiling. Each window had a set of cheerful curtains, freshly ironed and stiff with starch. Coal oil lamps that were filled and sparkling clean were fitted on brass brackets with polished reflectors ... six in all ... one between each pair of windows. A wire nailed to the ceiling supported a gasoline lantern, with ragged mantles, that would be used on special occasions.

The desks looked a little like the ones at Mason School. Made of smooth maple, each bore the scars of a Barlow knife and the carved initials of budding romances of the previous occupants. The old recitation bench was about eight feet long, made of 1 x 4 pine boards nailed about two inches apart. It had been polished by the seats of calico dresses and blue denim overalls for many years. The bell rope, with a long loop in it, was too short for all but the teacher and a few big boys to reach.

The teacher, with her new name, was seated behind a crude desk. She wore a pretty white blouse with a wide ruffled collar. Two wide straps over her shoulder were the same color and material as her skirt. Later Mom said it was a "jumper." Her contagious smile used all of her pretty face. I thought I could see a "halo" around her glossy hair. She was everything that Mom said she would be.

So on September 16, it was love at first sight ... and the beginning of one of the happiest school years of my life. The nine o'clock bell ended the scramble for choice seats. I had learned from the last year's experience: if you wanted a good seat, you had to be there early on the first day of school. However, Mrs. Hobbs and I didn't agree on the back seat I chose. I was moved to the third seat from the front on the north side. This was some improvement over last year though . . . when it was the first seat. Somehow I didn't experience the strangeness and the uncertainty this year. I had been in school before and felt more mature . . . I sorta looked down on the first year kids that didn't know much.

The sharp sumac and sassafras stobs left by Mr. Hearn's mower when he cut and burned the summer growth of brush and briars kept me close to the school-house during recess. I just ate one of my big Jonathan apples . . . and talked over big deals with some of the other barefooted boys.

At lunchtime I was seated on the limestone step by the door; when I pried the lid off my syrup bucket dinner pail with my pocket knife, right on the top of the sweaty sandwiches and fried chicken was that big red apple. I had a sudden urge to give it to Mrs. Hobbs. With boyish embarrassment, I approached her. I told her I would like to share one of my apples with her. Without palaver, she gave me a wonderful smile and a most gracious "thank you."

I walked away from her pleasant smile with a feeling of satisfaction and the greatest sense of well-being that I had ever known. As the warm sunny September days rolled by, I was enthralled by Mrs. Hobbs and I never ceased to admire her.

On the way home from school a few days later, I discovered a big hollow oak stump in Job's Woods. It was nearly three feet in diameter and about waist high to me. The hollowed-out area was larger than a bushel basket. The bottom had a soft cushion of decayed wood pulp. This would be a good place to hide some apples . . . so I lined the stump with sage and tickle grass.

Finally, Mom and Dad sacked all the windfall apples and sold them to the vinegar plant. The good apples were picked and sold in baskets. Because of oversight or being out of reach, several nice apples were left on each tree. The warm days and cool nights made them turn a brilliant red. Each morning when I walked the path through the orchard, I would watch for leftover apples. When one would drop at night, I would dig it out of the grass and store it in my secret stump. By the time frost came, my stump was full. I filled a burlap sack with some corn shucks and stuffed in the top of the stump to keep my apples dry and to keep them from freezing when it got colder. I never went to my secret stump the same way twice . . . a path might have given my secret away.

As the school term rolled on, I shared my apples with Mrs. Hobbs often. She accepted each one without fanfare but always with a warm smile and a gracious "thank you" which were reward enough. I never rebelled at anything she asked me to do nor did I ever resent anything she told me. Once I sassed her; she threatened me . . . said I had disappointed her. That broke my heart and I vowed that I'd never sass again.

The apples didn't last long, but the memories have.

The lane behind the barn

THE COUNTRY CUPBOARD
A RENDEZVOUS WITH NATURE

"In the beginning God created . . . the earth. And God said, Let the earth bring forth grass, the herb yielding seed, and the fruit tree yielding fruit after his kind, whose seed is in itself, upon the earth: and it was SO. And the earth BROUGHT forth grass, and the herb yielding seed after his kind, and the tree yielding fruit, whose seed was in itself, after his kind: and God saw that it was GOOD."

—Genesis, Chapter One

Of course, it is not given for all to live in the hills and big timber country, but blessed are the folks who have felt the call to the hills . . . and responded.

Here in the Ozarks, there is no finer way to get close to nature than to mosey along an old briar-bordered cow-path on an early spring day and watch the good earth in her travail giving birth to new life.

It is soul-stirring to get a glimpse of the fleecy white blooms of the wild goose plum, the vivid pink of the red bud, and the creamy waxed petals of the legendary dogwood clinging to the limestone and shale ledges framed with the aromatic, dark wintry-green cedar and with a backdrop of dormant feathery gray forest slowly yielding buds to a warm beckoning spring sun.

Earth-shaking thunder and blinding lightning, ushered in at night by heavy spring rains, split tree after tree in their wrath. Rain, whipped with a relentless wind, falls in sheets, drenching the greening earth with its life-giving fluid, floods down the hillsides muddy from the erosion of unprotected soil, water from opposite hills meeting at the bottoms of the ravines in mob-like violence rushing and leaping toward the creeks with a defenseless cargo of leaves, dead brush, poles and logs leaving huge drifts on all but uprooted pawpaw, mayhaw and willow trees.

The following morning the rain-laden leaves are sparkling under the shafts of a bright morning sun that are sifting through the closely woven branches. A stir caused by a soft south breeze, burdened with the fragrance of chinquapin, black locust, and wild grape, brings shower-like water from the leaves of the vine-enshrouded trees and underbrush.

While trudging along the wilderness aisles on a thick carpet of dead leaves, one can hear the deep muffled crunch, feel the give of breaking twigs under foot and the hot beaming sun bringing the musty odor of molding leaves and decaying dead fall from the damp ground. Following a narrowing ridge which ends abruptly, there is a high limestone ledge overlooking the forks of the creek below and a narrow hollow which widens with considerable irregularities into a friendly and serene valley. Several shaft-like spirals of blue wood smoke rise aimlessly from clapboard-covered cabins forming a thin blanket-like cloud just beneath the crest

of the pine-studded hills. The cabins are surrounded by deer-proof paling fences. A narrow winding gravel road ties the cabins together and disappears into the bend of the valley.

The familiar, rhythmic tool of several cow bells as the cows leisurely chew their cud, the boastful crow of a rooster, the cackling of ambitious hens, the listless bawling of a hound on a cold fox trail, the nicker of a lonesome horse, a woodpecker impudently hammering on a dead snag with rivet-hammer rapidity, the bold clear whistle of the cardinal as it flashes from tree to tree, the noisy jay (bluer than the sky) cocking his head defiantly at all intruders, the diminishing babble and the laughing chatter of a receding creek—all add to the peace and serenity of the valley.

While the hills are green with spring, we think nothing can be more pleasant and satisfying but now comes the time of ripening. The hills are brooding beneath the summer sun; most of the wild blossoms have come and gone. Their wild fruit are in many stages of growth. Some have already ripened and gone; others will ripen in mid-summer; still others will ripen nearer frost time.

Now oak-shaded springs are shrunk to mere trickles and ooze through beds of watercress and strong horse mint or disappear underground. The leaves begin to have a tired look, having lost their waxy luster. Now the days are getting shorter; the nights are getting longer and cooler. A suggestion of autumn is in the air. Everything seems mature; the air smells different. The ravines and valleys have a misty blue haze. The fall sun is farther south; its rays lengthen and slant the bulky shadows of the westward hills far to the north. The lonesomeness of the night comes early with the gloom. It is evident that summer is losing its battle to an oncoming winter. All signs point to an early frost.

The day is chilly and damp. A cold mist is falling intermittently, driven by a stinging northwest wind. All the hill folks are scurrying about picking green peppers and tomatoes, covering late vines and plants with sacks and baskets. In late evening the clouds break apart and a red sun sinks from a clear sky, the wind dying with it. The dawn of a new day finds white crystals covering the fertile earth; with one bold stroke almost all vegetation is put to sleep for the winter. In a day or so, nature, rich in her choice of colors, splatters the dingy oaks with vivid Oriental hues.

This rugged wilderness is populated, for the most part, by a hardy mountain people with a wealth of knowledge and understanding of the great out-of-doors. The rifle and an unerring aim have furnished the family

The favorite fishing hole

table with wild game. The turbulent streams of clear, cold limestone water cascading down deep-cut gorges have supplied fish. Wild edible fruit gathered from the off-beaten paths of the wilderness aisles grace the table with jellies and preserves. Succulent shoots of polk, dock, lamb's quarter, sheep sorrell, water cress, and skunk cabbage have supplied greens and salads. In many cases the bark, leaves, roots, and seeds of wild herbs have provided his beverage. A sharp axe and an iron muscle have given him the roof over his head and fuel to warm and cheer his cabin.

While an ever-expanding modern world has made constant inroads on the mountain way of life, much of it remains the same today as it was when the Divine Master brought it into being on the evening and morning of the third day.

Occasionally because of a late spring frost, drought, early frost in fall or perhaps for some other reason, we will lose one or more of the wild fruits; but usually a good variety is left, but oh, so hard to get. The old settlers are about gone with their large families, those we used to depend on for the crop; about all the old folks have passed on and many of the young folks have been driven from the old homestead by drought and hardship, leaving behind their heartaches, clapboard-covered cabins and rotting fences.

The first 16 years of my life I lived on the edge of the river breaks and the big timber country; having the only phone meant that the people could and would come at all times of the day and night to summon help, a doctor, etc. It meant our humble home must never be locked (and as far as I know not one single thing ever came up missing). Mom always felt it her sacred trust to soften the blow of fate. As a result, those wonderful people, who lived in homes where the word *convenience* was unknown, whose income was so meager, whose needs were so great, and yet in whom greed was never evident and selfishness and jealousy were rarely observed, shared with us all their heartaches and problems.

Across the years we learned to appreciate these noble people. We have encouraged them to harvest these nature-enriched wild fruits in season. They bring them to us in buckets, baskets, tubs, boxes, or what-have-you. We wash the fruits and put them in large cans; then they are frozen to retain all their natural nutrition that only a virgin soil that has never been touched by plow or hoe, can produce—frozen until they are needed for jelly and preserves. Then and only then are they thawed and made into jelly and preserves . . . sorta like you would at your house.

In the next few paragraphs, I would like to help you to understand how these wild fruits look and where they grow. It must be remembered that every wild fruit has its place in the wonderful plan of creation. Rarely do two fruits flourish in the same place or ripen at exactly the same time. For example: the mayhaw is at home in the

160

Wild Crab Apple

O'Possum Grapes

Paw Paw

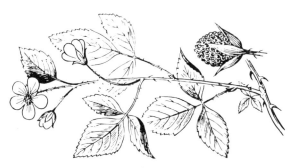

Dewberries

swamps, another fruit dangles from limestone ledges, others on rocky creek banks, and some on dry ridges. Some fruits ripen from spring 'til frost high in the tree tops, others on rambling vines on the ground.

The wild fruit season begins with the wild mayhaw ripening in May, as the name implies. A shrub-like tree with sprawling branches and a trunk rarely more than six or eight inches in diameter, it grows twelve to fourteen feet tall, usually sharing the woods with other trees much larger than itself. It grows in black gumbo soil near river banks and enjoys itself most when streams overflow. Legend has it that when mayhaw bloom while standing in water they will be gathered in boats when ripe. The fruit is about the size of a small acorn . . . dull red when ripe and fibrous in texture, has a pleasing fruity fragrance that permeates the air; it can be identified long before you get to the trees. When ripe and the streams are overflowing, the fruit is shaken from the trees and floats into improvised funnels and is dipped up with a minnow net. However, when the ground is dry, they must be picked by hand, a real job. Aside from the jelly, they are also used for butter.

Wild muscadines are characterized by their dainty leaves, rambling vines and temperamental moods (they do not bear every year). Muscadines have a thick skin and big seeds and grow three or four in a cluster about the size of tame cherries. Carrying a uniquely sharp flavor, they get ripe just before frost. Muscadine jelly and jam is a "must" in the pantry of every mountaineer's cabin. The muscadines are more at home in the South and Southeast, beginning in the swamps of the Carolinas and running westward into East Texas. They do grow in other regions, but not as consistently. There's lots of work in a gallon bucket of muscadines.

The Ozarks have at least two varieties of wild huckleberries: the high bush and low bush; low bush is considered best quality. Huckleberries grow on rocky

Wild Mayhaws

Wild Goose Plum

Wild Gooseberries

ridges in small patches about the size of a small house and on bushes about knee high. The fruit turns red as it matures, then dark blue when ripe and ranges in size about like a string of pearls. They are stripped from the bush. They make better jelly and preserves when mixed with a few green ones . . . more tart . . . and are a great delicacy when used in cobbler or fresh pie.

Dewberries are an old favorite among the natives. Their sprawling vines armed with wicked briars running along the ground are usually found in open areas such as pastures, fields, and lanes, sheltered by wild grass and weeds that have been deserted by livestock because of the severe briars. The vines grow six or eight feet long. The berries, when ripe, are about the size of a man's thumb and almost black in color. They have an interesting flavor, much different than that of their kinfolks.

The blossom of the wild goose plum is about the size of a cat's paw and is one of the most fragrant of all wild fruit blossoms. It is one of the first to bloom in spring. Legend says that a hunter once shot a flying wild goose and when he picked it up, a plum seed fell from its crop. He planted the seed . . . and that is where the wild goose plum came from. This plum grows on scrubby bushes in thickets, does best in fence rows, deserted home sites, along ledges and isolates itself from other trees somewhat. Goose plums are about the size of a turtle dove egg and shaped a little like a peach . . . bright red in most cases, but in some instances a real pleasing yellow. They are "mouth-puckering" sour (except when dead ripe) and a most sought-after fruit for jelly, preserves and butter. This early bloomer is always subject to frost and freezes and misses often.

Wild cherries grow on a real pretty tree with small smooth leaves and a smooth bark that appears waxy. Cherry trees range in height from ten to 100 feet, prefer wide open spaces, like to be alone and to share their friendly shade with livestock. The lumber made from

Wild Elderberries

Wild Blackberries

wild cherry is used for making expensive furniture. Wild cherries grow in bunches like 'possum grapes and about the size of garden peas . . . mostly pit . . . black in color, with a fine "pitie" flavor; when the wild cherry is used in alcoholic beverages, it is called "cherry bounce." We are forced to share the fruit in the top half of the trees with the birds. Wild cherries are tedious to pick . . . man's work.

The wild elderberry is as traditional as the farmhouse itself . . . likes to grow in large clumps along fence rows and other out-of-the-way places. The tiny blossoms are off-white and fleecy. The wild elderberry groups itself into a large round head about the size of a small dinner plate. The fruit, when ripe, is about the size of huckleberries. Other than jelly they are used for making wine. The elderberry shrub had a pithy center and will be remembered by many for the paper wad pop-gun that got them into trouble with the teacher.

Wild summer grapes, sometimes called "fox" grapes as many of you know, grow mostly in damp ravines and hollows near creeks and branches . . . thriving on dark rich soils. Their long vines ofttimes capture the towering oak, black gum and sycamore trees along the lower levees of the Mississippi, White and St. Francis rivers. This purplish blue fruit is about the size of small marbles and grows in bunches high up from the ground . . . sure enough hard to get, but worth the effort when made into jelly.

Wild blackberries probably grow over a wider area than any other wild fruit but are never harvested in large quantities because of the hot weather, chiggers, ticks, and vicious briars. The vines grow from three to five feet high in patches along seldom-traveled trails, ditches, abandoned orchards and fields . . . usually sharing their place with tickle and sage grass, sumac and sassafras bushes; they make a natural hiding place for rabbits, quail and other small game birds. They make them feel

Muscadines

Wild Huckleberries

Wild Summer Grapes

Wild Cherries

more secure than in any other place. Blackberries are about the size and shape of a blue jay egg. When vine ripened . . . they sure are good with heavy cream and sugar.

'Possum grapes are another member of the grape family but have their own wilderness personality . . . not as widely grown as their kinfolks. They are found occasionally on dry ridges. The ripe fruit is dusty black and near the size of garden peas but does not make a good jelly until after frost.

Wild gooseberries are native to the Ozarks but not as plentiful as other wild fruits . . . usually found in woodland pastures along ledges and rim rocks. They do not require as much sunlight as some other wild fruits. The vines are two or three feet high and have a tender briar. I think that the gooseberry is related to the currant. They are picked after they are mature but still green and tender . . . very tedious to pick and stem for canning and preserving. They are used for pies more than any other way.

There you have it . . . the country cupboard of jellies and preserves carries with it the rich spirit of the past in a fine rural atmosphere and represents a way of life that is rapidly vanishing from the American scene.

LANDMARKS OF GOOD EATING

The memories of youth are everlasting but become exaggerated and richer with the ceaseless flight of time. Deep in the recesses of every mind, there is a strong sensory image of childhood kept tender by the everyday experiences of growing older. Sometimes the slightest vestige of a childhood experience may evoke a warm memory richly laden with thoughts of yesterday.

Sometimes I like to think about yesterday . . . review the landmarks and episodes that shaped my childhood. I remember my life as being uncomplicated, peaceful, and serene. It seemed that everything I wanted though was a long way off; hope and anticipation were the forerunners of the real thing. I looked forward to getting something almost as long as I have remembered getting it. I discovered that it was an accumulation of many pleasant, though insignificant, experiences that made life worthwhile.

Do you remember when huntin' and fishin' were a way of life and not a sport? Fishing tackle was a hook, line, and sinker wrapped around a cork and carried in your pocket. The rod was fashioned from a long limb or a cane pole cut from the cane brakes when you reached the creek. Flies and spinners were wiggling worms in a can. You strung the catch on a forked limb.

There was a time when markmanship could be measured by the number of squirrel tails hanging out of your pocket or your neighbors knew how many quail you got by counting the shots. The bag limit was as many as you needed and no more. You discovered early that—regardless of how crisp and brown the fish were fried—they tasted better if you caught them. No matter how good squirrel and dumplings were cooked, they tasted better if you did the shootin'. The quail were better eatin' if you did the feather pickin'.

The sweat and toil of a family farm was a way of life too . . . not a hobby or a tax loophole. We were specialized farmers all right; we specialized in survival. When we outwitted frost, flood, drought, and insects, we recognized this as an achievement. Aside from the proper sunshine and rain, we needed little. We got our substance from the breast of nature; she fed, clothed, and sheltered us. We knew of only one obligation: to our Creator on whose land we farmed. Mom and Dad walked and talked as free and independent people, and that they were, calling wrong, wrong and right, right . . . as it seemed to them, and without fear of reprisal.

Life, at times, seemed harsh. The length of a day's work was governed by the sun instead of the clock and all too often we used a lantern to stretch both ends of the day. The day had its rewards though: rest, real rest . . . not from tension and fatigue but from tired weary muscles . . . a bountiful table of food that we had planted, plowed, and harvested brought straight from the field to the kitchen and prepared by the skilled hands of a mother who knew how to feed hungry folks.

Like most family farms we had the family cow, Maude,

who wasn't the cow that kicked over the lantern that started the Chicago fire—so she was never known outside of our neighborhood. She wasn't distinguished with a pedigree either ... she didn't even have a number ... but she did have a personality. She also had a calf every fall, a sweaty nose, and an enormous appetite. Maude was as much a part of my daily life as Carlo, my dog.

It was my job to milk and care for Maude morning and night; to do so 365 days a year was a trial of patience. In spring and summer I pulled weeds and grass to supplement her pasture. She was given all the bad heads of cabbage, tough lettuce, sweet corn stalks, and bean vines as a bonus. In fall and winter I fed her corn fodder, mowed oats and sudan grass with a dessert of turnips and culled sweet potatoes. She would eat anything that she could chew and swallow ... and tons of it. It was just like filling a silo. Maude had an outgoing disposition that endeared her to our family. It was through her generosity that I had all the milk, butter and cottage cheese I could eat, and I liked the stuff.

One of the landmarks of the season occurred in May of each year. A rich lady would spend a month in her summer house, near our house, to rest and can strawberries. She engaged a quart of milk every day ... seven quarts a week ... four weeks ... 28 quarts at seven cents a quart delivered ... $1.96 and all mine.

I am not sure whether I lived before or after the ice wagon or maybe we just lived too far out of town. At any rate the only thing I knew about that was frozen and good to eat was ice cream. Maude could provide the milk and cream, an old hen the eggs, but the ice was something else. So ice cream was rare at our house. If we had it at all, it was Saturday night, a few times in summer. Dad would buy a block of ice when we left town, put it in a burlap sack and wrap it in an old quilt to avoid too much melting. I would milk Maude the minute we reached home, then beat the ice to pieces with a pole axe, fill the freezer with milk, cream, eggs, sugar, and vanilla extract, chuck a layer of ice and a layer of salt, layer of ice, another of salt and so on until it covered the freezer good. Then I cranked for dear life—until it was too hard to turn. I always looked forward to licking the paddle. The only thing wrong with homemade ice cream . . . if I ate too fast, it made my head ache.

Being an ex-boy myself, I can speak with great authority on the subject of good eatin'. Before I was an ex-boy though, parents accused boys of being "hollow clear down to their toes," claiming they were in constant danger of "being eaten out of house and home." Just an ordinary day started out with breakfast, not a ⅝-ounce box of cereal, but a real meal. I'm talking about home-cured bacon, more than a couple of slices too, eggs, at least two, a glass or two of Maude's milk that tested five or six per cent butterfat, biscuits usually . . . but sometimes a few slices of homemade light bread loaded with pure home-churned butter and toasted in the hot oven of a wood-burning range, then smeared with a quarter of an inch of homemade strawberry preserves. When you got up from the table you were fortified—not for all day—just 'til noon . . . then there'd be dinner, not lunch. In the spring and early summer, it would be a big kettle of navy beans that had been soaked overnight, then cooked all morning with a big hamhock the size of your two fists . . . skin and fat on the outside, red meat and bone in the middle but enough red meat for everybody. There was a big bowl of wild greens that included poke, wild lettuce, lamb's quarter, sheep sorrel, dock, and skunk cabbage. They had been picked the day before ... washed ... blanched ... seasoned with bacon rinds ... then simmered on the back of the stove 'til dinner time. A batch of stone-ground cornbread baked in too large a pan so it would be thin and crusty ... about 20 or 30 minutes of this and you were fortified again ... 'til chore time. For supper, not dinner, it would be a kettle of blackeyed peas seasoned with bacon fryings and corn-on-the-cob with melted butter running down between the kernels, and a slice or two of country-cured ham. For dessert, a cobbler ... with a golden brown crust ... dished out into an oatmeal bowl and covered with thick folds of handskimmed cream. It was about as close to heaven as you could get and still have your feet on the ground. Did we overeat? ... lands no. Following a team of quick-stepping horses between the two handles of a walking plow solved the calorie problem ... you did well to last a half day.

There are many special occasions and landmarks of good eating—take the old-time pie supper, for instance. They were at least two-fold in purpose: to raise money for a poor school district for one thing and to have some homemade fun for another.

Mr. Sweet owned the ice plant in town; he was considered a rich and generous man ... always wanted to help the country schools around Siloam Springs, so he was always invited to our pie suppers. When the time came to give the cake to the prettiest girl (based on a popular vote of one cent each), Mr. Sweet gave the boys a real race. He would select a fine girl but not necessarily popular. We boys would put up our prettiest girl, sometimes two or three to start with. He would raise the ante just enough to keep the voting lively and finally he would let us win by the skin of our teeth, but only after the most of our money was gone. In those days a girl was esteemed more for the pies she baked than the style of clothes she wore. Bidding on pies would get serious at times, especially if two or more boys had a crush on the same girl. I was far more interested in the pie than I was in the girl, so I was there early and got a good look at the pie boxes as they arrived.

Mrs. Hearn was a fine lady . . . a good pie baker and usually I could bid in her pie for thirty to fifty cents. I can think back and count fifteen or twenty romances that budded at Bellview pie suppers, but I remember how Mrs. Hearn's chocolate pies tasted best of all.

The grain cradle and the horse-powered threshing machine were before my time . . . it was the big steam tractor with huge steel wheels, tall smoke stack and a roof over most of the platform and boiler that provided that power that separated the grain and blew the straw into big stacks that would feed and shelter livestock, come winter. As I look back now, I still think I would like to have been the engineer or separator boss, but the nearest that I came to it was riding the water wagon and helping eat threshing-day dinner.

As I recall, it required 20 to 25 men to make a crew—

farmers trading work. Some of the women folks always came along to help with the dinners . . . sort of a work trading proposition, too. Just about every housewife tried to outdo her neighbor and certainly didn't want to be accused of being stingy, so when her time came to feed the crew, she went all out to do it up right. At our house it was fried chicken and ham and lots of it . . . gallons of chicken gravy and ham gravy, boiled cabbage and sour slaw, wilted lettuce, blackeyed peas, green onions, radishes, cold milk, coffee and nine-inch lemon and apple pies, cut in quarters, and chocolate cake, too. One thing every farm wife knew: the threshers couldn't pitch big bundles of wheat for a half a day without at least two helpings of everything.

Brother Scroggins, our pastor, preached at the Gum Springs Church the second Sunday of the month and had for as long as I could remember. And Sunday, May 11, became another landmark in good eating to me.

This was the year the ground hog failed to see his "shadder," so spring had come early to the mountain country. Garden and field had yielded to a warm sun and gentle showers, leaf lettuce was ready to cut, long white icicle radishes were sweet and crisp, the fresh pea pods were crammed with tender peas, new potatoes were as large as hen eggs, and three acres of strawberries were ready to deliver the first shortcake.

Two of our accommodating Rhode Island Red hens had decided to set in early February. Mom assisted each with 15 well-chosen, pencil-marked eggs. At the end of 21 days, it happened—just as it has happened since

Often the harvester was also the consumer.

the beginning of time—they hatched: 23 downy, buff-colored chicks as cute as Mother Nature could shape them. Eight roosters and six pullets survived the spring rains, hawks and all the other hazards of a chicken's life. By early May lots of buttermilk-soaked yellow corn-meal had changed all eight roosters from cute, fluffy chicks to 4½ pounds of awkward, long, yellow-legged chickens whose future was already determined. The only question left was when; this Saturday, May 10, would be the day for the first one I could catch.

It was a busy time to invite the preacher for Sunday dinner with all the pea canning and strawberry picking at hand, but Mom thought that Christianity could best be measured by personal sacrifice, and she was willing to do just that even if it meant staying home from town on Saturday to hull peas, scrape new potatoes, bake bread and dress chicken.

If going to Sunday school or church then had been as easy as it is now, the churches couldn't have held the people. Going to church was a serious matter in those days. You arose as early Sunday morning as any other morning. Sunday clothes were worn only on Sunday; at our house there was only one outfit to choose from. Dad had the suit he was married in . . . it was heavy and hot in summer . . . he thought of it more as a lifetime investment than the way it looked. Mom always expected more from her corset than she should, but it did make her dress look nice and I suppose that made it worth a half-day of torture.

I went barefooted all summer; when time came to put on shoes and stockings for Sunday, the religious mood of our house was reduced somewhat. It felt like coals of fire in my shoes. My shirt was always starchy and as stiff as a joint of stovepipe . . . always made red streaks around my neck. All this and a scratchy pair of pants made church-going a real sacrifice to me.

Gum Springs, a landmark for thirsty travelers, was a never ending stream of cold, crystal clear water running from a hollow gum stump then trickling through thick beds of dark green watercress and mint and along the rocky road apiece and finally disappearing into a deep ravine on the way to the river.

The white frame church that bears its name was organized about 1896 and has changed the lives and helped to direct the course and destiny of many people. The Gum Springs church sat on the side of a hill overlooking the spring and the rocky road . . . surrounded by big virgin timber; inside, the church was neat, clean, and plain. The pump organ was one of the church's proudest possessions. The pulpit was barely large enough to hold an open Bible. The benches were simple, too, made from plain lumber and didn't accommodate the natural curves of the body very well. The backs were straight and low; this discouraged sleeping when the preaching was close and someone tried to sleep off a guilty conscience.

Brother Scroggins was a good man and lived what he

preached; he was also a part-time farmer and he knew how to talk farm folks' language.

Sunday morning he would preach from what he called a "heart of love" and would describe heaven in such a way you could see the gates of pearl and feel the golden streets under your feet . . . made you really want to go there someday. On Sunday night it was different: when the windows were open, you could hear him way out in the timber. He preached with great conviction and evangelistic fervor. He told the folks it was a Christian's duty to uphold the law, back up the church's high moral standards and help make the church a refuge for lost sinners that were wandering through a wicked world. He pointed out in no uncertain terms that sinners could expect punishment for their wrongdoing. There were times when I could almost smell burning brimstone. He convinced me early that I wanted no part of wrongdoing. The only thing wrong with Brother Scroggins . . . he was long-winded.

There was an advantage in going to church early on Sunday, especially when Brother Scroggins preached: folks could get their visiting done before church . . . thus an earlier dinner.

We arrived at the church early this particular morning and tied Molly to her favorite tree. Brother Myers had just finished ringing the nine o'clock bell. A few men were sitting on their heels whittling and discussing crops, stock, etc. A cluster of women was standing near the bottom steps of the church visiting and eyeing a new dress or two, and the kids were too clean and too uncomfortable to move much. A few minutes after we joined the group the sweet mellow notes of the old pump organ floated through the open windows to receptive ears and the folks walked toward the church. We were given Sunday school literature dated May 11, 1922.

Brother Scroggins preached earnestly and convincingly. The gospel fell on fertile soil; it was evident the hearts of the folks were attuned to his message. And most of the folks were of reasonable thrift and shared their substance when the offering plates were passed.

It was after one o'clock when we reached home. I was starved. Mom said dinner was ready except making the gravy and mashing the potatoes. My first glimpse of that table made me wish Brother Scroggins would come every Sunday. Right in the middle of the table was the big platter of chicken, sprinkled generously with black pepper and fried to a golden brown . . . right on top a thigh as big as my fist and a leg almost as long and big as an ear of corn (I knew Brother Scroggins would get one or the other), surrounded by a bowl of fresh peas swimming in a sweet cream sauce, a gallon milk crock half full of wilted lettuce, a round mold of yellow butter, a tray of green onions and radishes, a boat of milk gravy with chunks of chicken fryings the size of my thumb and strawberry shortcake that would be topped with whipped cream after a while.

To a growing boy, it's a long time from 5:30 in the morning 'til 2:15 in the evening. When Dad asked Brother Scroggins to say the blessing on the food, he must of misunderstood because he asked the Lord to bless the world, the missionaries, the churches everywhere, the rich and the poor, the good and the bad, our home, his home, and finally the food. By now, I had passed the point of human endurance . . . besides the gravy was getting thick. Up to now, this was one of the few times I had eaten at the first table when we had company. I discovered there was a difference.

The small farm, the family cow, the watermill, Mason jars, home canning and preserving are about gone. The joy of the harvest is all but unknown to millions. The rural school and church surrounded by the village store, blacksmith shop and a few dwellings are no longer the community centers. With them went a way of life that will not return.

To those who grew up during the period of the family reunions, big wood sawings, neighborhood butchering times, camp meetings and all the other events that included the good things to eat, it is pleasant to recount landmarks in our memories.